ESCAPE
VELOCITY

ESCAPE VELOCITY

How Narrative Immersion Can Revolutionize Reading Education

JAMES FLANAGAN

First published in the United States by Contrapposto Press

Escape Velocity: How Narrative Immersion Can Revolutionize Reading Education

For information about this title or to order other books and/or electronic media, contact the publisher:

Contrapposto Press
www.contrappostopress.com
contrappostopress@gmail.com

First Edition: July 2021

ISBNs:
978-1-7363830-2-5 (hardcover)
978-1-7363830-0-1 (softcover)
978-1-7363830-1-8 (eBook)

Printed in the United States of America

To our kids, who deserve better

CONTENTS

INTRODUCTION

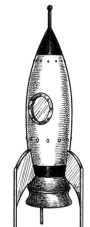

What is it for a human life to go well? The answer, I believe, is that living well means meeting the challenge set by three things: your capacities, the circumstances into which you were born, and the projects you yourself decide are important. Making a life, my friend the philosopher and legal scholar Ronald Dworkin once wrote, is 'a performance that demands skill,' and 'is the most comprehensive and important challenge we face.' But because each of us comes equipped with different talents and is born into different circumstances, and because people choose their own projects, each of us faces his or her own challenge, one that is, in the end, unique.

~ PHILOSOPHER KWAME ANTHONY APPIAH

Given that children grow up with different talents, circumstances, and interests, how do we as educators help each one meet his or her unique challenge in life? How do we give children a distinctively personal education through which they can develop their capacities to the fullest, improve their circumstances, and gain the freedom to follow where their curiosity leads them? How do we accomplish this and simultaneously impart essential academic skills? Achieving these goals is difficult in any case, but it is particularly so when one of the circumstances is concentrated poverty. Poverty can hinder the development of talent and limit the pursuit of interests. Faced with such obstacles, how can educators give children the personalized education that they need?

Germantown Avenue in Philadelphia represents the full spectrum of economic circumstances our children are born into. Starting with concentrated wealth at the top of Chestnut Hill, you can wind your way down Germantown Avenue into the concentrated poverty of North Philadelphia. In *Code of the Street*, sociologist Elijah Anderson documents the complex structural confines of the high-poverty end of Germantown Avenue. He details the deft code-switching required to navigate the contrasting worlds along the street as well as the limited helpfulness of code-switching. He shows that frequently the need simply to focus on survival in a desperate environment precludes any ascent into the middle-class.

Researcher Susan B. Neuman has investigated the economic variation along Germantown Avenue as well. She reveals how this broad material disparity translates into a dramatic print disparity. Our affluent neighborhoods have an abundance of high-quality books in their homes, bookstores, and well-funded libraries. And she shows how our low-income neighborhoods primarily have low-quality reading materials such as coloring books available in dollar or drug stores, and austere libraries with limited hours. Neuman writes about a polarity so complete, with poverty so concentrated, that she describes certain locales in Philadelphia as "book deserts."

It's comforting to believe that we live in a meritocracy with class fluidity. Yet, as Neuman states, "spatial concentration of poverty and affluence . . . virtually guarantees the intergenerational transmission of class position." Faced with stark environments and a rigid social stratification, our neediest children face severe odds. Sadly, our meritocracy is a myth: Without the tools to achieve merit, children cannot be rewarded for it.

Prominent among such needed tools are books. Educator Rudine Sims Bishop has written that books are both mirrors in which we see our personal experiences reflected and windows through which we gain access to new worlds. To succeed academically and personally, children need exposure to high-quality literature, but children from homes with a scarcity of material resources, including appealing books, face a corresponding scarcity of opportunity. Reading is a practice—without practice, there can be no achievement.

Of course, reading proficiency depends on more than the quality and quantity of available books, but this material deprivation has a resounding impact. Deprived environments contour us socially, emotionally, and intellectually, often culminating in a diminished socioeconomic status. Children living in poverty are bound by virtually insurmountable structural restraints, and becoming a highly-effective reader is one method to loosen them. If we can equip children with high-level reading skills, we can give them a means of self-development and self-advancement that will benefit them throughout their lives. We need a practical classroom model that allows all students—but especially those from impoverished backgrounds—to build the best life possible by voraciously reading their way into advanced literacy.

Each classroom is a unique and complex system. It is a collection of autonomous, novelty-seeking, idiosyncratic personalities operating within the constraints of the curriculum, high-stakes testing, and a school culture. And it is up to the teacher to integrate these motley components smoothly. Reading education is frequently unsatisfying and flawed because it is deeply complex and multifaceted, and thus easy to manage badly. Just having a large classroom library of great books is not enough. Just having engaging read-alouds is not enough. Just having extra time to practice reading is not enough. Just letting the students read what they like is not enough. Piecemeal efforts will not have a significant effect. Changing a system this complex requires a comprehensive strategy that is also feasible in a real-world classroom. Highly significant results require balancing all of these elements properly and successfully integrating them into a school day.

When you live a precarious life in concentrated poverty, isolated from resources and opportunities, you focus on daily survival. You do not have the luxury of immersing yourself in high-quality reading experiences when you live in a book desert. Yet, there is a way to address this deficiency and to disrupt the inadequate education too many of our students receive. We can create and provide what the outside environment cannot. Individual classrooms can be the elementary particles of change. By exposing students to good books, we can genuinely engage and rigorously challenge them. Our classrooms can address critical human needs such as social inclusion, novelty, and freedom. We can build classroom environments that simultaneously provide a cohesive community and also give each student the freedom to follow where his or her curiosity leads.

We can mitigate inequality in our individual classrooms. We can compensate for students' material disadvantages by providing immediate access in the classroom to a large volume of high-quality, high-interest books with diverse characters by diverse authors. We can build trusting relationships with our students by spending quality time together in read-aloud sessions exploring high-level, thought-provoking texts from diverse traditions. We can support the development of strong reading proficiency by providing substantial time and guidance to practice independent reading. And we can empower our students by letting them select from a rich array of literary texts that mirror their own experiences and allow them to explore new experiences that stimulate their curiosity.

If we provide autonomy, access, and enough time to practice, our students can become highly-skilled readers. This, in turn, will help disrupt the intergenerational transmission of social and economic status. If we shift our focus to intrinsic motivation, if we build authentic relationships through inherently meaningful storytelling and dialogue, if we build a classroom environment where trust and cooperation are taught through captivating works of the imagination, we can meet the fundamental literacy needs of our children and help support a thriving educational system.

However, not just any stories will do. Author Philip Pullman has postulated that certain stories are superior to others because of the specific type of wisdom they transmit. The superior story asserts that if you are unhappy with the way things are, you should refuse to accept it and attempt to improve it. The superior story instructs us to not wait for anyone to save us, because we need to find the solution ourselves. And the superior story declares that those solutions require us to be creative, determined, and resourceful. Superior stories instruct us to embrace bravely the reality of this mostly terrible world and unyieldingly attempt to improve it through our action and wits.

What is it for an education to go well? If what Kwame Anthony Appiah says about life generally applies to education, then it cannot myopically focus on generic utility and acquisition of skills. We inherently crave novelty, joy, and discovery. Not just the privileged—but all of our students—need classrooms that emphasize individual curiosity, freedom, depth, and differentiation. When we neglect these intrinsic drives, the result for many students is an uninspired, narrow, stunted academic life—virtually ensuring their permanent underprivileged status. Equal access to a quality education is the gateway to a better life. The fate of a stifled life, squandered potential, and unnecessary suffering of children living in poverty is not sealed. The superior story tells us there is a way out—we need only to act.

• • •

CHAPTER 1

MAKING MEANING

We do not receive wisdom, we must discover it for our-
selves, after a journey through the wilderness which no
one else can make for us, which no one can spare us, for
our wisdom is the point of view from which we come at
last to regard the world.

~ MARCEL PROUST

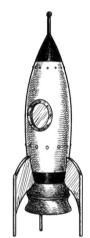

FUNCTION VS. PASSION

magine being taught basketball drills five days a week, and trained exactly the way the coach wants, but without any creative agency. Imagine never having the choice of whom to pass to or when to shoot. Imagine being diligently taught the rules from the rulebook, and completing drills year after year, but never being given the time or freedom to play the game for enjoyment. Imagine being repeatedly evaluated and tested. The joy of basketball is in the aesthetic performance of the game, the improvisational creativity, the tension, the freedom to make decisions, the camaraderie, the community. The joy of reading lies in these things as well.

Extrinsic, artificial drills will not nourish you. Most of us would quit before progressing to an advanced level. But what if the focus of your practice was playing authentic games? We can create superior readers by infusing joyful expression into our reading instruction and laying the groundwork for intensive practice through authentic engagement.

Year after year, I noticed a dominant trend in my classroom. Most of my students disliked reading and read primarily for functional purposes, while a select few seemed to read out of passion. This recurring dichotomy seemed a strong indicator of present and future academic achievement.

The function-readers knew how to read words, but outside of facilitating the completion of school work, didn't ascribe much value to it. They viewed reading as a tool for completing assignments and nothing more.

The passion-readers discovered reading could bring gratification beyond utility. The passion-readers would independently seek out new books, and even choose reading over screen time. The passion-readers were switched on and awakened to the facts that they have the capacity to ask questions that are personally meaningful and that they have the capability to search for answers through books. They discovered agency and were empowered to attend to what is meaningful to themselves and to explore those possibilities through narrative. The passion-readers wrote better, were more accurate in solving math word-problems, used a more sophisticated vocabulary, and read with more fluency and comprehension. Even in those as young as ten, you could see the contrasting paths students were embarking upon based on their reading facility. It appeared that every year I taught, I would have a class of function-readers and a handful of passion-readers. I wanted a systematic intervention to invert that ratio.

Reading enhances your life in a multitude of ways. In order to excel academically, you need to be a proficient reader. We generally teach kids how to read, but not how to be readers. Focusing on creating function-readers as opposed to passion-readers in school is a mistake. Under the guise of rigor, we can discourage students' joyful engagement. If executed properly, rigor is positive. Misapplied, it is destructive and counterproductive to the learning process. Unfortunately, I think rigor is often misconstrued with joylessness. However, if you are rigorously engaged in something you love to read, something that is not merely academically instructive, the experience is unmistakably joyful. Rigor and joy are not mutually exclusive. We should be challenging our kids on a day-to-day basis to rigorously practice passion-reading.

We need to escape the cognitive bias of targeting function-reading improvement. Function-reading is tedious and only improves function-reading while diminishing the motivation to read. And every time we diminish the motivation to read, we are decreasing the likelihood of the student practicing independent reading—an activity we know increases reading ability. Passion-reading on the other hand increases enjoyment, boosts the motivation to read, and improves function-reading all at the same time. As Stephen Krashen has written, "The single factor most strongly associated with reading achievement—more than socioeconomic status or any instructional approach—is independent reading." We need to correct the narrow focus on function-reading in our schools and balance that with opportunities for independent reading, so that all children can become high-level readers.

JOY AND STORYTELLING

Joy may not be a required component of a curriculum, but we should not underestimate its impact in our classrooms. Joy in the classroom looks like a combination of interest, engagement, and contented delight in the moment. But optimal joyful engagement is more than just having a warm, pleasant atmosphere; it is also a dynamic motivator for learning. The experience of losing oneself in a challenging activity is transformational. Achieving this flow state and being completely absorbed in what you are doing is known to be helpful in countless activities and disciplines. It works just as well in nurturing passionate and successful readers. Being absorbed in a story and successfully reading a story go hand in hand.

When we help children experience sustained engagement through reading, it motivates them to return again and again to reading as a source of joy. It encourages them to practice and improve their skills repeatedly out of a love for the game. Mastery requires thousands of hours of deliberate practice. A few minutes of silent reading and a teacher occasionally reading aloud a few stories will not create a passion-reader. We need to make a daily, sustained effort to be able to flip that switch and enable the transition. We cannot overestimate the motivational power of joyful reading experiences. Every time a student is internally motivated to return to a book, it initiates a positive feedback loop—amplifying his or her learning. Whether it is a teacher reading aloud or an author transmitting silently with written words, sharing well-told stories with someone is emotionally powerful and joyful. And we should be taking full advantage of this power to energize instruction. Harnessing the enjoyment of a good story in education is simply capitalizing on one of our most distinctive human attributes.

Whether experienced personally during independent reading or communally during a read-aloud, the enjoyment of literature is about growth. It is about eagerly extending yourself, extending your world, and extending your relationships with others. What is learning, if not growth of this kind? Whether physical or intellectual, growth is not something that can be imposed from without; it can only be nurtured, guided, and given the room it needs. Students need structure and seek novelty, and they desperately want to learn. As adults, our job is to provide them with opportunities to learn about ideas, people, and places that pique their curiosity and to provide an academic environment that will help this engagement develop into advanced skills and knowledge.

When we simply push knowledge on students, we treat them as passive vessels, and numb them to school. Alternatively, when we recognize students as active meaning-makers—each with highly specific, unique, intrinsic motivations—we give them the opportunity to follow their innate curiosity to answer questions personally meaningful to them. Their learning is accelerated through the joy of self-guided discovery.

Tedious instruction and too much screen time may make children appear dull, but our children are neither passive nor indifferent to learning. Beneath that sometimes jaded veneer, every child is passionate about something, and that something will frequently not be represented in the curriculum. Our children need the guidance and opportunity to express that passion. Every child is a potential passion-reader; we only have to jostle that reader free by consistently nurturing his or her latent curiosity.

Michelangelo said that every block of stone has a statue inside of it, and that as a sculptor he was only helping release it. We should not be attempting to chisel the students into what we think they should be. We should be apprenticing them to be master sculptors of their own lives, assisting the release of their fully developed selves.

The essence of teaching is helping someone learn how to improve his or her life. The most effective way to achieve that is by creating a passion-reader who through reading is empowered, has self-efficacy, becomes braver and more disciplined, and can reflect critically on the world around—all while gaining through literature knowledge and understanding of worlds that are new to them. Joy, art, and love are the things that make life worth living, and while they can be found in many places, they are readily available in books. As a teacher, you are constantly adapting your instruction, tweaking your pacing, and over-hauling your curriculum. All of these adjustments are beneficial, but they don't always improve learning as much as we would like. If you can take advantage of an entire school year with a child to turn that child from a function-reader into a passion-reader—permanently—then you can change everything.

There is an effective way to bring about this change. Research makes the case for self-selected, high-volume reading. And there is an uncomplicated way any teacher or school can implement a robust reading program that incorporates these strategies. Such a program can be implemented by ordinary teachers operating with ordinary budgets. It will not require them to find additional hours in their crowded schedules, simply to make the most effective use of it. Even without extraordinary resources, we can achieve the extraordinary goal of turning function-readers into passionate ones.

WHY PASSION-READING AND MEANING-MAKING MATTER

The Way It Is
~ WILLIAM STAFFORD

There's a thread you follow. It goes among
things that change. But it doesn't change.
People wonder about what you are pursuing.
You have to explain about the thread.
But it is hard for others to see.
While you hold it you can't get lost.
Tragedies happen; people get hurt
or die; and you suffer and get old.
Nothing you do can stop time's unfolding.
You don't ever let go of the thread.

In his poem, "The Way It Is," William Stafford writes of a unique thread we each have. This thread is difficult for others to see. Everything around us is guaranteed to change, but our thread will remain constant. He writes that it's essential to understand this thread and to never let go of it. To some degree, we are all untranslatable. Within us, there are contours only we ourselves know. And you can't determine for someone else what they find meaningful. Yet, in school, children are given little, if any, say regarding what is significant to them. Children deserve the dignity adults take for granted of deciding for themselves what they find personally meaningful. As teachers and parents, we need to support both their freedom to choose and the choices they make.

The critic Kenneth Tynan comments that Samuel Beckett's "Waiting for Godot" is ultimately about "passing the time in the dark." Tynan goes on to say that passing the time in the dark is not just what Godot is about but what *life* is about. We stumble into life, find our bearings, adjust course, and hopefully find our way through the darkness. Stories are the candles in the darkness. They light our paths and illuminate our experiences with meaning. Stories allow us to benefit vicariously from lives that are not our own but that may resonate powerfully with ours.

I would add that, for too many students, school is also about passing the time in the dark. They have questions that they are never given the opportunity to explore. Science writer Elizabeth Kolbert identifies the defining characteristic of modern humans as our "compulsion to explore." This compulsion to explore explains our fascination with stories and why we need them. It is through stories that we process the world. By increasing the number and variety of stories we encounter and add to our mental repertoires, we improve our processing of the world.

When we are given the freedom to pursue answers to our own questions, when we are free to contemplate not only universal ideals, but also universal tragedies, we gain a fuller understanding of the world's beauty and agony. We are making meaning for ourselves in the only way possible. When we combine several elements together into an overarching instructional approach I call *narrative immersion,* it allows us to have a critical dialogue with ourselves that can help us figure out what exactly it is we desire for ourselves and set expectations and goals for our lives. This happens not in a public sphere or under the influence of social media and cultural expectations but rather through attunement to the "thread" in Stafford's poem. This is what Jeffrey Wilhelm and Michael Smith describe in *Reading Unbound* as the all-important "inner work" that takes place when you read with full engagement.

> Thus far we've seen that our readers consciously employed their reading as a tool to do immediate and important work in the world. Reading helped our participants be better writers, better talkers and thinkers, and better gamers. It provided them with richer understandings of the world outside themselves. It also helped them do inner work.
>
> "Inner work," according to Jungian scholar Robert Johnson, "is the effort by which we gain an awareness of the deeper layers of consciousness within us and move to an integration of the total self." The unconscious, according to Jung, expresses itself through symbol, story, and feeling. Jung argued that the two primary modes the unconscious uses to communicate with the conscious mind are through dreams and imagination. Jung maintained that when we approach the unconscious and embrace its messages, cultivating our receptivity and response to the language of symbolism, we lead healthier, fuller, more wide-awake, balanced, and richer lives.
>
> The notion that reading can be inner work, a spiritual practice, a way to profound and deepened ways of growing as human beings is not a new idea. The rule for monasteries established throughout Egypt and the Middle East by the Coptic Saint Pachomius maintained that the candidates for monkhood "shall be compelled to read." Benedictine rule likewise sets aside a period each day for "prayerful reading."
>
> The understanding that reading can provide an avenue for personal growth is something we've long argued for both separately and together. We've drawn on Wayne Booth's argument that "We all live a great proportion of our lives in a surrender to stories about our lives, and about other possible lives." Readers are able to learn about possible lives because, as Booth explains, stories are typically centered on characters' grappling in some way or another with moral choices. In living through those efforts,

> *"we readers stretch our own capacities for thinking about how life should be lived." Bruner makes a similar argument, claiming that narratives allow one to traffic "in human possibilities rather than in settled certainties."*

When I think about how important passion-reading is, I'm reminded of the research of Edward Deci and Richard Ryan, who suggest there are three universal human needs:

1. Autonomy—being in control of your own destiny, self-determination

2. Relatedness—a connection to others, belonging, experiencing love, and affirmation

3. Competence—pleasure from learning new things, acquiring skills, and putting them to use

When schools neglect these universal human needs, students suffer academically as well as personally. We shouldn't be surprised that students seem disengaged when the school gives them little control over their activities and little connection to others. According to Deci's and Ryan's research, disengagement is only to be expected. We are wired to make meaning in our lives, and joy compels us to action. In too many schools, we are not harnessing this human desire to make meaning or giving students permission to investigate the unique questions each of them has. There is joy in the pursuit of meaning, and we are failing to capitalize on it.

FLOW AND AUTOTELIC ACTIVITIES

The research of Mihaly Csikszentmihalyi sheds even more light on properly formatting your reading instruction. Csikszentmihalyi's book,

Flow: The Psychology of Optimal Experience, details the experience of the "flow state." The flow state is total involvement with life, and learning to find control amid chaos. If you can control your interpretation and inner experience of the world, you will to a great extent determine the quality of your life.

> *Over the endless dark centuries of its evolution, the human nervous system has become so complex that it is now able to affect its own states, making it to a certain extent functionally independent of its genetic blueprint and of the objective environment. A person can make himself happy, or miserable, regardless of what is actually happening "outside," just by changing the contents of consciousness. We all know individuals who can transform hopeless situations into challenges to be overcome, just through the force of their personalities. This ability to persevere despite obstacles and setbacks is the quality people most admire in others, and justly so; it is probably the most important trait not only for succeeding in life, but also for enjoying it as well.*

When you experience flow, you find the present moment intensely rewarding, and you do not feel bored or anxious, or worried about failure. In his lifelong research into the flow state, Csikszentmihalyi has discovered certain conditions which lend themselves to attaining this optimal experience. First, it must stem from intrinsic motivation—your unique personal makeup shapes what your mind attends to. You are only truly invested in goals when you yourself have chosen to pursue them. Flow is not effortless pleasure, but rather your full concentrated attention. You become so single-mindedly focused on the task that you, in effect, become the task.

Boredom is a negative experience. Anxiety is a negative experience. We want our children's experience of school to exist in the positive "flow channel" where they continuously encounter meaningful challenges.

Like Vygotsky's "zone of proximal development," where there is a perfect balance between challenge and manageability, but not over the edge to frustration—flow is about finding just the right level of challenge for your personal level of skill.

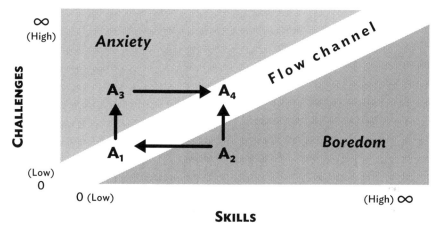

FIGURE 1-1: *The Flow Channel*

Csikszentmihalyi writes, "In flow a person is challenged to do her best, and must constantly improve her skills." The flow experience is one of "deep concentration, high and balanced challenges and skills, a sense of control and satisfaction" and "has the potential to make life more rich, intense, and meaningful." We need to help children find complete enjoyment in pushing themselves to new, higher levels of performance. If we focus on improving the quality of the school experience, we can increase our children's capacity to learn.

> *Again, the importance of personally taking control of the direction of learning from the very first steps cannot be stressed enough. If a person feels coerced to read a certain book, to follow a given course because that is supposed to be the way to do it, learning will go against the grain. But if the decision is to take that same route because of an inner feeling of rightness, the learning will be relatively effortless and enjoyable.*

Csikszentmihalyi highlights the significance of "autotelic activities." Autotelic comes from the Greek roots *auto*, meaning self, and *telos*, meaning goal. It refers to an activity done not for extrinsic reasons but because it is itself rewarding. "The autotelic experience, or flow, lifts the course of life to a different level. Alienation gives way to involvement, enjoyment replaces boredom, helplessness turns into a feeling of control, and psychic energy works to reinforce the sense of self, instead of being lost in the service of external goals. When experience is intrinsically rewarding life is justified in the present, instead of being held hostage to a hypothetical future gain." Csikszentmihalyi goes on to outline the major components:

> As our studies have suggested, the phenomenology of enjoyment has eight major components. When people reflect on how it feels when their experience is most positive, they mention at least one, and often all, of the following. First, the experience usually occurs when we confront tasks we have a chance of completing. Second, we must be able to concentrate on what we are doing. Third and fourth, the concentration is usually possible because the task undertaken has clear goals and provides immediate feedback. Fifth, one acts with a deep but effortless involvement that removes from awareness the worries and frustrations of everyday life. Sixth, enjoyable experiences allow people to exercise a sense of control over their actions. Seventh, concern for the self disappears, yet paradoxically the sense of self emerges stronger after the flow experience is over. Finally, the sense of the duration of time is altered; hours pass by in minutes, and minutes can stretch out to seem like hours. The combination of all these elements causes a sense of deep enjoyment that is so rewarding people feel that expending a great deal of energy is worthwhile simply to be able to feel it. We shall take a closer look at each of these elements so that we may better understand what makes enjoyable activities so gratifying. With this knowledge, it is possible to achieve control of

> *consciousness and turn even the most humdrum moments of everyday lives into events that help the self to grow.*

Too many schools do not honor students' natural inclination to learn about what personally motivates them and what they genuinely care about. Why should we teach against the grain, when we can accomplish much greater things through autotelic learning? And how do you maximize the efficacy of those nine months in the classroom? You establish a desire for autotelic learning so strong that it will remain with students throughout their lives.

THE INTANGIBLES

> *And the point is, to live everything. Live the questions now. Perhaps then, someday far in the future, you will gradually, without even noticing it, live your way into the answer.*
>
> **~ RAINER MARIA RILKE**

Research and common sense tell us quite simply that the more you practice reading, the more you improve it. And the better you get at reading, the better your chances of academic success. However we measure academic success, we see a positive correlation between time spent practicing reading and achievement. Data collection is important and should inform our choices, but we should not neglect the intangibles which exist beyond quantification. The tangible figures are only one side of the coin. The intangibles that passion-reading provides are just as—if not more—important, and yet they are frequently left out of account when we design our school schedules and curriculum.

When I look around a classroom and see students fully immersed in their books, books they personally selected for their own specific interests, I don't see them merely as improving their comprehension, fluency, and vocabulary—though that is certainly happening—instead, I see children asking and answering their individual questions. I see children searching for their better selves. There is nothing frivolous about passion-reading. It is a high-stakes venture, one that provides several intangible benefits.

1.   Intellectual Flexibility

An evolutionary biologist might say the most successful species are the species most adaptive to change. Couldn't we say the same thing about human success? In order to be successful in school and in life, you must have a high degree of mental flexibility. You must be mentally and emotionally agile in the world. It would be an adaptive advantage to have familiarity with as many potential situations as possible. This would allow you to game-out scenarios in your mind, however unlikely, that you might possibly one day encounter in real life. This is why the military conducts war games. Considering situations before they occur allows for smarter decision-making in the future. There is tremendous value in learning to think creatively about solutions, and this goal is not served by the convergent thinking we typically find in the classroom; it requires instead divergent thinking in the exploration of new possibilities.

2.   Broadening Empathy

You develop empathy when you read about another's life and slip into that person's perspective. By revealing the similarities that connect us and the commonality in our struggles, while yet bringing into relief the unique characteristics of each individual's experience, reading awakens connections to others that we might otherwise never have recognized. This empathetic reading experience makes us more compassionate toward others. As Rebecca Mead has written,

> But there are pleasures to be had from books beyond being lightly enter-
> tained. There is the pleasure of being challenged; the pleasure of feeling

one's range and capacities expanding; the pleasure of entering into an unfamiliar world, and being led into empathy with a consciousness very different from one's own; the pleasure of knowing what others have already thought it worth knowing, and entering a larger conversation.

We are born into one perspective, one viewpoint, and breaking free from this self-absorption is redeeming. It allows us to suspend our own ego and consider other vantage points. We broaden our perspective and awaken to other potentialities. Our life specifics are unique, but the arcs are the same. Philosopher Peter Singer has referred to this process of broadening our empathy as the expanding circle. The further you extend your circle of empathy, the more inclusive you become. Reading facilitates a reconsideration of tribal membership and expands our empathetic circle. He explains:

Our ability to reason can be a factor in leading us away from both arbitrary subjectivism and an uncritical acceptance of the values of our community. Reason makes it possible to see ourselves in this way because, by thinking about my place in the world, I am able to see that I am just one being among others, with interests and desires like others. I have a personal perspective on the world, from which my interests are at the front and center of the stage, the interests of my family and friends are close behind, and the interests of strangers are pushed to the back and sides. But reason enables me to see that others have similarly subjective perspectives, and that from "the point of view of the universe" my perspective is no more privileged than theirs. Thus my ability to reason shows me the possibility of detaching myself from my own perspective and shows me what the universe might look like if I had no personal perspective.

When my ability to reason shows me that the suffering of another being is very similar to my own suffering and (in an appropriate case) matters just

as much to that other being as my own suffering matters to me, then my
reason is showing me something that is undeniably true.

We are all limited by our own biographies. We have only one life and one body. Reading stories about other people, from another life perspective, helps us rediscover our position in the world. We triangulate ourselves through others. Other people's stories help us understand not only them but also ourselves.

3. Refuge

When you are given the freedom to lose yourself in another world through literature, you can challenge your mettle and perform the inner work that Smith and Wilhelm describe. This inner work provides guidance and ballast for the more difficult struggles that life presents. Writer George Saunders has spoken about the friction of being separate in the world and how painful it can feel, and he maintains that reading temporarily bridges the gaps we feel separating us from others. School (and life) can be taxing, and entering a calm, peaceful, safe place where you can focus intensely and build your intellectual skills is not only academically beneficial but is also a powerful antidote to stress. Learning how to relax quietly with a book gives a student a peaceful refuge from a trying school day.

4. Life Rehearsal

One morning during independent reading, an excited Aaliyah pops her head up in front of my desk and blurts, "I know what I want to be!" I ask her what that would be, and she yells "A baker!" When I ask her what made her decide that, she tells me she was just reading "Close to Famous" by Joan Bauer and that "Being a baker sounds cool. Foster went through a whole lot, but baking helped her and she just kept on baking. She also earned money and she's only twelve." Completely unprompted,

Aaliyah was just so excited about this thought that she wanted to share it with me. Maybe she will one day become a baker or maybe not, but the fact that she contemplated this future life, one that she imagines will make her happy, has given her energy and maybe in the process taught her a few life lessons from Joan Bauer about steps Aaliyah might take to get to this life she envisions.

Reading goes beyond simple enjoyment—it teaches you strategies for how to cope and survive. As children, we build schema based on what we've been told, taught, and shown. Living a life limited strictly to our native environment dims and obstructs our view. Reading allows us to explore beyond those schematic walls our environments have constructed, to traverse false boundaries, and to expand our frontiers. Popular culture is geared toward making us comfortable and is unlikely to challenge us, but stepping outside one's comfort zone is necessary for growth. This growth is the task of education.

Independent passion-reading dismantles false boundaries. It reminds us that life is not predetermined. We have agency. We have options. We have choices. We are not the prisoners of our circumstances. Every other assignment I give as a teacher pales in comparison.

When you allow students to choose their own books, you notice their choices frequently reflect their specific life challenges. I find one of my students with an autistic family member engrossed in *Anything But Typical* by Nora Raleigh Baskin, which is about a boy with autism. I notice one of my students whose mother just passed away tearing through the entire Harry Potter series, which explores Harry finding meaning in life despite the loss of his parents. One of my students, who has communication problems, tells me her favorite book is *Out of My Mind* by Sharon Draper, which is about a brilliant girl with cerebral palsy who has trouble communicating. It's impossible not to draw conclusions about why they love the books they do. And if we had never implemented this narrative immersion, they would never have had the access, time, or freedom to read those books.

Stories allow us to explore not only the world but also ourselves. And that exploration will challenge previously held assumptions, force us to reexamine and reshape those assumptions, and finally to reintegrate them into our ways of thinking. You have to be able to imagine and rehearse new ways of thinking before you can take the real-world steps necessary to achieve them. We struggle to find our roles in life and in the world, and reading allows us the freedom to try on different personas. You have to find the thread of belief in yourself and learn to push through challenges and persevere for existential reasons that matter to you and not for external rewards or acknowledgement. You have to learn to trust yourself in order to live with authenticity. Stories can give us the reassurance and the courage to believe in ourselves, even when we do not have others around us who do.

When I look around my classroom and see every child deeply involved in reading a book he or she selected for specific reasons of their own, I feel enormous gratification. Reading is the flight simulator of life, and my students are actively contemplating how to manage present and future challenges. When you read and engage intellectually with hundreds or even thousands of stories about challenges, you are preparing yourself risk-free for real world challenges. Reading stories tells us that we are not alone and that problems are surmountable. Children must have the freedom to explore their questions now if they are to ever live their way into the answers.

• • •

CHAPTER 2

BUILDING RELATIONSHIPS THROUGH READ-ALOUD

O ne of the most gratifying things about teaching is seeing the value of your effort. You can see the joy on a child's face when they figure something out for the first time or produce a piece of writing that they are proud of. You can also see the pain when they work hard and struggle and still fail to make the necessary connections. In my teaching I have noted a consistent pattern: children who are passion-readers are the ones who make the most connections in their learning and produce the strongest work. The function-readers, for whom reading is unrewarding and tedious, always have the most difficulty. It has become clear to me that finding a passion-reading "switch" within each child makes the difference between success and failure.

From a child's perspective, the task of learning how to read fluently is a hard one. Struggling to master a series of disjointed, mysterious rules that you must apply at progressively faster rates, so you can read literature that is mostly irrelevant to your situation, is not a process likely to make you love learning. Fortunately, though, there are proven methods for effectively engaging, inspiring, and transforming kids from function-readers into passion-readers.

I have found direction in the work and research of Richard Allington, Anne McGill-Franzen, Penny Kittle, Kelly Gallagher, Regie Routman, Stephen Krashen, P. David Pearson, Nell K. Duke, Thomas Newkirk, Jeffrey Wilhelm, Michael Smith, Debbie Miller, Barbara Moss, and many others. And I have found practical advice and inspiration in the classroom techniques of Nancie Atwell, Donalyn Miller, and Jim Trelease. They have shown me a research-based method of reading instruction and how to succeed at implementing it. Their knowledge and expertise have been invaluable in building and sustaining my reading instruction.

My ultimate goal as a teacher is to help each student lead the most fulfilling life possible. I know that literacy skills are paramount and that they not only help kids achieve greater academic success, but also help them discover new possibilities and find greater satisfaction in life. After years of focusing on skill instruction and nudging children toward literacy, I have come to realize that my efforts—no matter how persistent—would never be enough to turn a child from a function-reader into a passion-reader. I saw that there would always be an outlier or two in my class who fell into the passion-reading category, but I knew that a handful of outliers just isn't good enough. All kids can experience the joy and freedom that reading brings if we create the right conditions for that passion to grow.

Narrative immersion really grew out of personal dissatisfaction with my impact as a teacher. My enthusiastic classroom promotion of literacy by itself was never enough to inspire passionate readers. That was never going to happen by me extrinsically imposing my passion for reading onto the students. The only way to create such a reader is by nurturing a love of reading within each child individually. My literacy pep talks and constant promotion of reading during class were simply impotent against the forces of popular culture. You have the kids for such a limited time during the day; how can you compete with the rapid-fire bombardment of stimulation from video games, television, and social media? The deeply focused pleasure of reading is very different from the media culture in which our kids grow up. Most days it felt like Don Quixote tilting at a windmill, but as reading has taught me—some desperate causes are worth fighting for. In this fidgety, hyperactive media culture, making the time for daily introspection and focused reserve is difficult, but that's what reading requires.

I wanted to maximize my impact so that my students could improve their odds against a stacked deck and find a way to flourish. I realized that if I was going to have the impact I desired, I was going to have to make something grow that would not die in June. I was going to have to give my students some type of intrinsic motivation that would last long after they left my classroom. I would need to set into motion a positive feedback loop that would reward, renew, and increase motivation year after year.

30 MINUTES OF DAILY READ-ALOUD

If you treat an individual as he is, he will remain how he is. But if you treat him as if he were what he ought to be and could be, he will become what he ought to be and could be.

~ GOETHE

Whether your school uses restorative practices, responsive classroom techniques, or some other classroom model, gathering together as a community is essential. The read-aloud is the family dinner of the school day. It is where the soft skills are taught. It is where we discuss issues together, check in, model, and show concern. Too frequently our school days are dominated by hard skill instruction, which, if not complemented with joy and connection, reduces engagement. The daily read-aloud is about modeling reading for pleasure and enrichment and helping students progress to more sophisticated levels of comprehension. Read-aloud builds foundations for gradually giving students more responsibility. Slowing relinquishing control, allowing the child to make more and more decisions with the hope that he or she will then eventually become a fully formed, responsible adult.

My daily read-aloud session consists of three things: curation, exposure, and modeling. The curation element is the teacher staying on top of the newest titles, researching the best read-aloud books, and acquiring them for their class. The exposure element is reading from a broad variety of poetry and prose, allowing students to experience high-level content that may be beyond their own reading skills yet accessible through the spoken word. The modeling element is demonstrating what good readers do when they read by thinking aloud, rereading significant passages for better comprehension, and delivering the story with appropriate prosody and expression. Many students have too little experience with what a great story sounds like when read aloud, and we should provide that experience. Reading-aloud is about letting them rise above their independent reading level, because when the words are delivered carefully and expressively, students can understand.

You can read books in read-aloud that might be too difficult for the children to read on their own, stretching them to higher levels and introducing them to more complex thoughts. Because the books are at a higher level, you are exposing students to more complex ideas as well as language and, while more sophisticated books can contain inappropriate content or language, you can just skip over those parts. So reading aloud ostensibly consists of curating, exposing, and modeling; however it is, in fact, much more than that. The read-aloud session is where relationships are built. It is my opportunity to demonstrate empathy and compassion and to see those things reciprocated. It is beyond statistics or algorithms. The entire foundation of my classroom management is the 30 minutes every morning when I connect with my kids, sitting with them at eye level and reading aloud to them. It's where we show each other respect, share stories, laugh, empathize, and, ultimately, bond. Going in cold to a classroom without knowing the kids and trying to teach is almost impossible, because you haven't built that relationship yet. The story-telling, humor, compassion, and joy of the read-aloud forge this bond, and that bond is essential to our success as a class. If we all want to be in that classroom together, we all will perform better. This camaraderie may be hard to quantify, but it is indispensable.

Why do we love listening to stories so much? I think listening to a good read-aloud is equivalent to watching an NBA player dazzle with the grace and excitement of a beautiful basketball play. It is inspirational to watch someone who is talented perform. The teacher reading aloud is the exemplar and demonstrates what reading should sound like inside your head. If you have never marveled at the sheer joy of a well-told story or a deftly performed game-winning shot, how would you ever know what you're striving for? Both are pleasurable, instructive, and inspiring.

A successful read-aloud session has three segments: poetry, prose, and book talks.

POETRY

I love starting the day with our read-aloud, and I love starting our read-aloud with poems. The economy of the language is what gives poetry its power. Reading poetry is the verbal equivalent of the slow-motion replay in basketball. You can easily miss what is happening until you slow it down enough and focus on the constituent elements. Reading poetry every morning to the children—deliberately unrolling one word at a time—showcases the potency of language. Poetry is the concentrated power of individual words working together to create original thoughts and attempting to express the inexpressible. When we slow language down, we can start to fully appreciate it.

Poetry teaches us that words matter. An example of how much words matter is a joke my colleague Mr. Giorno and I started playing on our students. The joke was based on the idea that there is a tendency in education to obfuscate instruction unnecessarily with bafflegab language. At the beginning of the year, we dryly informed the kids that we don't have recess in fifth grade, but we do have something called "constructive socializing." We explained that constructive socializing is based on healthy, positive engagement with your classmates and the objective is to build relationships as a class. They were allowed to play whatever games they chose, as long as they paired up with at least one other person, immediately welcomed anyone who asked to join their game, and avoided any destructive arguing or animosity (which would end the constructive socializing time).

It started as an inside joke between us teachers, and we delivered it seriously to the kids, but the crazy thing is that those two words completely shifted expectations and behavior. We saw the members of the class step in and squash disagreements that started to get disrespectful, we saw kids dial back their own snarky comments, and we saw the kids warmly welcoming their classmates into different games. And because the kids knew that the better they got along as a class, the more constructive socializing time they would have, in a genuinely funny way they would sometimes behave in an ostentatiously friendly manner toward each other. This would make everyone in the class laugh and create even more good will. Together those two words completely redefined how our kids viewed what was formerly called "recess." Constructive socializing started as a silly joke, but it stuck, and we have used it consistently for years. I think the connotation of *recess* is that anything goes, and the connotation of *constructive socializing* is that you are going to hang out together in a fun, positive way, and no one in the class will be excluded. So words and labels matter enormously, and poetry beautifully illustrates this power.

Poetry, wonder, and human connection matter now more than ever. In a world where you can literally ask a question aloud and a digital device approximates an answer in response, it's important to preserve what poet John Keats called "negative capability." He describes it as "when a man is capable of being in uncertainties, mysteries, doubts." I interpret this as not being frustrated by the mysteries of life, but finding balance in the pursuit of happiness and marveling at the wonder of the world. It means stoking the curiosity behind the questions we all have and realizing the answers aren't delivered by a machine-generated voice. When technological advances are hyped to offer pat solutions and remedies, we need to preserve space for wonder. We need to secure time to ponder the mysterious and to develop a flexible, adaptable mind.

I find a lot of poetry abstruse or confusing, so it is important for me to curate my selections and try to find the gems most likely to speak to the heart in plain language for my students. At the same time, it's also important to resist the urge to dissect the poem. To paraphrase Yeats, if you can explain it, then it's not poetry. I find it helpful to provide some background context and highlight what appears to be the theme. I want to expose students to a broad variety of thought, so they can discover what it is they might prefer and what personally speaks to them. Poetry to me invites a kind of philosophical mindfulness. When finding definitive answers usually drives the school day, reading poetry creates some room to ponder questions.

To provide some context, I think it is helpful to highlight the major theme or important metaphors in the poem. But once we begin to make the poem too much of an academic exercise, we kill it by dissection. Just as you tell a joke but don't explain why it's funny after you tell it, you can read a poem without needing to explain it to know its power. Explanation might only serve to dilute its power.

I recently read to our class poet Natasha Trethewey's set-up to David Kirby's poem "Taking It Home to Jerome." She writes, "The phrase that

David Kirby's DJ utters, with its mystery and sonic pleasures, reminds me of the way a poem can work: how its language can say one thing and mean another, and how we can be moved by the musicality of words, finding meaning in their sound."

Taking It Home to Jerome
~ BY DAVID KIRBY

In Baton Rouge, there was a DJ on the soul station who was
always urging his listeners to "take it on home to Jerome."

No one knew who Jerome was. And nobody cared. So it
didn't matter. I was, what, ten, twelve? I didn't have anything

to take home to anyone. Parents and teachers told us that all
we needed to do in this world were three things: be happy,

do good, and find work that fulfills you. But I also wanted
to learn that trick where you grab your left ankle in your

right hand and then jump through with your other leg.
Everything else was to come, everything about love:

the sadness of it, knowing it can't last, that all lives must end,
all hearts are broken. Sometimes when I'm writing a poem,

I feel as though I'm operating that crusher that turns
a full-sized car into a metal cube the size of a suitcase.

At other times, I'm just a secretary: the world has so much
to say, and I'm writing it down. This great tenderness.

Natasha Trethewey's introduction is perfect. And David Kirby's poem is perfect. If I were to try and lead a thorough analysis of that poem, I would only diminish it. I read the introduction, and I read the poem. The space is there for the kids to share any feeling or thoughts they have about the poem. It's important to highlight the theme but not dissect away the magic.

I also talk about how poems can be like songs we love but don't fully understand. They can be like songs whose lyrics we may not know or understand but can feel and understand anyway. I play the Icelandic band Sigur Ros and tell the class how we may not even know the language of the lyrics, but we can understand the emotion. It's expressing the inexpressible. I casually mention the song "Can't Feel My Face" by The Weeknd and how I love that song and get it, without precisely knowing what the singer's not feeling his face with his girl means. But then I said if you really, really like it, that might make you want to investigate the song and the lyrics in more depth, for example, through a close reading of the lyrics. My student Lamin suggests that maybe the guy can't feel his face because he has hypo-thermia, and then Jason adds maybe he can't feel his face because his girlfriend is made of ice, or maybe because he is dating an air conditioner. These are not the interpretations I was expecting, but they are, nonetheless, hilarious.

Another powerful read-aloud poem is "Mid-Term Break," by Seamus Heaney, with its plain, beautifully delicate language. I preface the reading by telling them that Heaney wrote this poem about a real-life experience and that they should pay close attention to the poem and see if they can figure out what it's about. That way they get to discover the poem them-selves. After I read it, and the kids chime in with ideas and impressions, I read it aloud again so they can build a better understanding. Poems naturally teach comprehension, because they promptly throw you into the unknown and invite rereading.

Mid-Term Break

~ BY SEAMUS HEANEY

I sat all morning in the college sick bay
Counting bells knelling classes to a close.
At two o'clock our neighbours drove me home.

In the porch I met my father crying—
He had always taken funerals in his stride—
And Big Jim Evans saying it was a hard blow.

The baby cooed and laughed and rocked the pram
When I came in, and I was embarrassed
By old men standing up to shake my hand

And tell me they were 'sorry for my trouble'.
Whispers informed strangers I was the eldest,
Away at school, as my mother held my hand

In hers and coughed out angry tearless sighs.
At ten o'clock the ambulance arrived
With the corpse, stanched and bandaged by the nurses.

Next morning I went up into the room. Snowdrops
And candles soothed the bedside; I saw him
For the first time in six weeks. Paler now,

Wearing a poppy bruise on his left temple,
He lay in the four-foot box as in his cot.
No gaudy scars, the bumper knocked him clear.

A four-foot box, a foot for every year.

When you share a poem deliberating on real-life issues, and read it in a reflective, observant way, it opens the members of the class up to each other. Without prodding, kids then want to share the moments they found out a loved one had passed away and the small details they noticed, and the rituals that took place. No one is forced to comment, but many want to talk. They want to share their experiences. And the ones who prefer to just listen and comment appreciate the conversation as well. The morning I read that poem I had no lesson-plan containing the objective to talk about death. But that poem cracked open the door, and provided the space for an authentic conversation. We sat face to face and had a compassionate discussion as a community about life, death, and making sense of it all.

PROSE

Jim Trelease's The Read-Aloud Handbook *convinced me* to make time every single day for a pleasurable read-aloud with the class. And it was immediately apparent that the activity was the highlight of the day for my students. We gather around a table, sharing stories and poems that take us on journeys to faraway places and give us mysteries and parables to contemplate.

Though reading aloud is a perfect activity for meeting the Common Core Speaking and Listening standards, none of my students are worried about assessment during the read-aloud. Its purpose is sitting together as one tribe, opening the world up and collectively exploring it. It's a great way to start every morning. I huddle together with my students at eye level, able to connect with them and pick up who seems engaged, who seems distracted, who seems depressed or upset. I get a good sense of where the class is at and, if necessary, can use that sense to shift the book selection of the read-aloud. If something of significance has occurred in the school or in our nation recently, I can try to find the right story or poem to address the fear or elation the class may be experiencing. Teachers have influence over the emotional climate and general tenor of the classroom, and the read-aloud is the perfect opportunity to capitalize on that influence and strengthen those bonds.

What makes it so powerful for the kids is that they have the security of a predictable read-aloud routine every morning, and what keeps it fresh and exciting is that the predictable routine contains tremendous novelty in the variety of ideas. This format invites meaningful moments into the school day. In an objective way, you are teaching human values. The teacher is not dictating what to believe, but posing questions and sharing ideas from great writers and thinkers. For example, Jon Muth's picture-book version of Leo Tolstoy's story *The Three Questions* is an ideal prose selection for read-aloud. It considers the essential question of what is the best use of a person's life. And that question is explored in a profound, yet accessible, way. The protagonist goes on a quest, during which he discovers his answers. The most important time is the present, the most important people are the ones you are presently with, and the most important thing to do is to do good for the ones you are with. It's hard to argue with that. As a teacher, I am presenting well-considered writings, and then it's up to the class to formulate opinions and interact as a class.

Ultimately the read-aloud is about establishing not a teacher monologue but a community dialogue. It's about preserving flexibility and spontaneity in the school day through compelling narrative and allowing the individual members of the class to participate and influence the learning process. Since read-aloud is naturally Socratic in its posing of questions and sharing of thoughts, it eliminates the need for didactic lecturing; instead, we as a community—as Rilke said—live our way into the answers.

We need to concern ourselves with how students experience school just as much as we do with how they perform. Schools can be remarkably alienating places, and we need to build genuine connections to counter that alienation. Group dynamic research emphasizes the significance of groups having *psychological safety*. For any group to function at its highest level, its members need to feel accepted, respected, and safe enough to allow themselves to show vulnerability. Not only is a group happier and more cohesive in an atmosphere of *psychological safety*, but also the quality of its work improves as well. The daily read-aloud is integral in facilitating this atmosphere.

Sherry Turkle has written about the decline in our society of this type of conversational interaction. Our kids grow up in a technology-connected, humanity-disconnected world, and it isn't going away. As teachers, we cannot control what happens when our kids are at home. The lucky ones will sit with loved ones and share stories together, learn how to engage in warm conversation, and learn what it means to truly listen to each other. Too many kids, though, will miss out on this deep human connection. An internet connection is no substitute for a group of empathetic people welcoming you in.

But we can provide the family dinner of the school day—the read-aloud. We can spend time with our class establishing that kind of relationship and having that kind of dialogue. Every morning my students gather around, and I check in with them, check the emotional climate, see how things are going, and see if I need to immediately address anything. It is essential to establishing harmony and group norms and to determining our classroom values. I have selected stories to read that will introduce my kids to new authors, just as a family dinner would introduce children to new kinds of food. I have them extend their minds a bit, the same way at home they might extend their tastes. I curate the reading selections, I model how to read by thinking aloud and reading aloud, showing students how pacing and prosody work, and finally exposing them to new authors, stories, worlds, and ideas.

Unless you were raised eating delicious, healthy food, you don't know how delicious healthy food can be. The daily read-aloud does this job for literature. It allows me to model and demonstrate how satisfying a great story can be, and with this example before them, kids can start making healthy choices on their own.

The teacher modeling that happens during the read-aloud—together with the experience of stories that have ethical dimensions and present models of virtue—is not the same as the teaching of specific content. It is not about teaching *hard skills*. Instead it is about teaching the *soft skills* that are essential to living a happy, productive, examined life. It is about modeling respectful interaction with others in an authentically welcoming environment. It is about learning how truly to listen to and genuinely see other people when having a discussion. It's about sitting around a table and connecting with a community and not just consuming digital pablum.

Whenever I ask past students what their favorite memory from my classroom is, they invariably tell me it is the read-aloud. Why? Because there is an inherent warmth and connection when people gather together, look each other in the eye, and share stories. We are forced to confront each other's humanity. It is a daily ritual that starts the school day off in a comfortable, pleasant way. It is building a familial bond that we naturally and deeply desire. It allows the teacher to step away from an elevated position of authority and become more of an equal. The kids look back on those read-aloud sessions with great fondness and the reason they do is that those sessions were filled with trust, respect, laughter, and love.

BOOK TALKS

Mixing in book talks during the session is the perfect complement to the teacher reading-aloud poetry and prose. Everyone is already gathered around and focused, and having the kids share favorite books they have just finished or are currently reading gets them more actively involved. Especially for the more introverted students, quietly sitting together instead of standing in the front of the class is a less intimidating way and more comfortable way to interact and share their experiences with their classmates.

A great example of the significance of the book talk is something that happened with one of my shyest students. When the school year began, she was exceptionally timid and never spoke in class. Then, for independent reading, she selected *I Am Malala: How One Girl Stood Up for Education and Changed the World,* by Malala Yousafzai and Patricia McCormick. She did a wonderful book talk for our class, describing how much she loved the book and how much Malala inspired her. When it came time for our student-led Parent-Teacher conference, she presented a slideshow she had created for her mother of her favorite book. Here are excerpts from her presentation:

I Am Malala,
by Malala Yousafzai and Patricia McCormick

- The main character in the story is smart, funny, ferocious, and aware of everything. She doesn't want the Taliban not letting girls in her country go to school, so she tries to keep going to school.

- Malala is very smart when it comes to almost every subject, but speaking is what she is good at mostly, especially to other classmates and other moms when in groups for a meeting.

- Malala stood up for what she believed in, which is going to school to learn what she can. If you like books about awards and standing up for what you believe in then you would like this book too.

- This made me feel very courageous and made me feel like I have faith in myself to stand up for what I believe is right.

No test can measure the value of a perpetually down-looking, shrinking-in-her-seat, nervous little girl finishing the year as a stronger, more self-assured young lady. No number will quantify this change, but her progress was unmistakable. Such growth does not come from a single read-aloud session or a single book, but when you put 180 school days of cultivating a group dynamic of psychological safety through read-aloud sessions with 180 school days of autotelic learning where students read 40, 50, or 60 great books, remarkable things can happen. I'll take life prep before test prep any day.

• • •

CHAPTER 3

ENABLING ACCESS

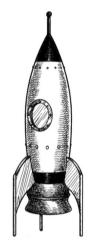

I like reading books, because it's like my mind just loves all the books that I read. When my eyes hurt, my mind is saying "Keep going, I want to know more." I keep on going.

~ DANIELLE R.

nspired by the work of Nancie Atwell and Donalyn Miller, my colleague Mr. Giorno and I organized our library by genre, exposed book covers to catch students' eyes, and greatly expanded our selection by going to book banks, library sales, and ordering online.

To engage the students, our classrooms need a large classroom library. Mr. Giorno and I found that having about a thousand books each works well. Different books speak to each of us, and there needs to be a wide variety that children can choose from if they are ever going to make the leap from function-reading to passion-reading. Even if we love to read and have wide-ranging interests, most books are simply not going to be that appealing on a personal level. Passion-readers know exactly which genres, writers, and subjects they find endlessly fascinating, and they know where to search for those books. A major impediment for students who are not yet passion-readers, though, is knowing where to find the books that would speak to them as individuals. Before they have a sufficient understanding of their favorite genres, writers, and subjects, students need us—their teachers and parents—to expose them to the magnificent array of reading possibilities that exist. Students need to be given the opportunity, time, and freedom to follow where their curiosity leads them before they can become passion-readers.

There are plenty of ways to acquire the books you need for your classroom, and local library sales and used book donations are good ones to start with. However, while there is nothing wrong with books being used, their appearance is important. While we know that words are words and that tattered pages shouldn't matter—they do. If you want students to get excited about books, you need to curate the condition of the books on your shelf as well as the books themselves. Children genuinely find fresh book covers with modern-looking layouts and intact pages exciting. They find new and newish books very attractive and are more likely to pick them up for a closer look. Even if the words on the inside are exactly the same, books that look fresh and gently handled invite the children to investigate. Judging a book by its cover is natural, and fresh books on the shelf are more welcoming to children's curiosity and exploration.

Of course, there are libraries. Libraries are amazing places that provide tremendous public benefit, but not all libraries are created equal. Depending on the school, libraries may not have a good selection of children's literature or be located where they are easily accessible for children. For many years, my colleague Mr. Giorno carried out a personal project to increase students' use of library books. He would pick up library card applications, have students take them home for their families to complete, return the applications to the library, and pick up the library cards when they were ready. Then he would schedule appointments with the librarians for visits, schedule the time with us fellow teachers who wanted to participate, and schedule the time with the administration so that we were approved for the trip on the school calendar. Finally, we would walk the three-mile round trip to the library.

As you can see, it required quite an effort to enable kids to have access to library books. It was worthwhile, because we were visiting the Central Branch of the Philadelphia Library System, which is well-stocked (and, as a cultural bonus, architecturally inspiring), and the kids were able to find great, high-quality books that appealed to their interests. Our school was fortunate to be able to participate in this project, and to have a teacher like Mr. Giorno willing to do so much extra legwork to make it happen, but the reality for most schools is that this kind of monthly field trip won't be feasible.

For schools lucky enough to have them, there are also school libraries. Students may be able to select new books every week and have a weekly visit with a knowledgeable librarian; but because of budgetary issues, many schools are losing their libraries or seeing them suffer from a deficiency of varied, interesting books. That is why the best solution is for students to have immediate access right in their classrooms to a very large collection of high-quality, high-interest books.

Teachers can increase the depth and range of their classroom libraries by teaming up with their colleagues and allowing any of their students to borrow from any of their classroom libraries. As teachers become more familiar with other teachers' collections, they can help students inquiring about specific titles by directing them to another classroom.

I have found it very beneficial to meet my kids in September and find out what their personalities are like through conversations, interest inventories, and conferencing. This allows me to discover what books they enjoy or might enjoy. By gauging their interests and then ordering books suited to these interests, I can tailor my library to my class. I know the kids appreciate that I am ordering books based on their interests. I also make sure I spread my money out over the year, so I can place several orders. Periodically refreshing our library reinvigorates students' desire to plunge into the stacks again and again.

It's not easy to build a large classroom library, but it's important to have a critical mass of high-quality, high-interest books available. When students are surrounded by books they are genuinely excited to read, it builds momentum for their reading goals. When they find not just one book that captures their attention, but fifty that do, it motivates them to read more, because they see fifty new adventures they want to experience.

When you bring colleagues into the project, you can potentially multiply the number of books available to students by the number of colleagues you recruit. My students borrow books primarily from me, but they are aware that other teachers have books that I don't, and that they are free to borrow from those collections as well. And my colleagues' students come into my classroom to peruse the titles I have. This interaction between classes helps build a free-flowing intellectual community among the students. They discuss favorite books and alert each other to particular titles in particular classrooms. They recommend new titles to each other based on what they learn of each other's interests. This interactive cross-pollination builds community between classrooms and allows students to find other kids in different classes or even grade levels who share their interests, favorite authors, and genres.

When you lend out so many books, some will disappear. It is frustrating to purchase specific titles for your library and then, when you look for one, to find it's gone. Despite your best efforts, some books will walk. It's the price you pay when you offer radical accessibility to compelling books. It's the price of literary free will. I have a sign-out sheet that kids are responsible for using when they borrow a book. They fill in their name, the date, the book title, and the price of the book. This requirement helps instill a sense of personal responsibility in the borrower in a way that is encouraging rather than threatening. The sheet is mostly for kids from other classrooms. The students in my class are in and out of my room every day and are pretty good about returning the books. If I start with a thousand books in my room, then by the end of the year I will probably have lost close to a hundred. Of course, I'd love to have those books back, but I can live with the trade-off. If you train your kids to read and bring books with them wherever they go, they will leave books wherever they go too. To have books for each classroom, classroom libraries need to be an item in every school's annual budget. Classroom libraries need yearly replenishment and periodic refreshing throughout the school year.

DISTRACTION-FREE COMFORT

What happens when busyness and sociability leave no room for solitude? The ability to engage in introspection is the essential precondition for living an intellectual life, and the essential precondition for introspection is solitude.

~ WILLIAM DERESIEWICZ

Homes and schools can be chaotic places. Some of this chaos may be beyond our control, but there is a tremendous amount that we can eliminate. The environment in which students read is extremely important. We need to do our best as teachers and parents to provide a warmly lit, cozy, silent, comfortable space so that our kids can feel calm and comfortable enough to forget their surroundings and drift away into their stories. The ambience of the classroom is important and worthy of the time and effort it takes to create a good one. We need to create the conditions in which students can fall in love with reading. There are a few things to which we need to pay particular attention.

When you go to the theater or the movies, they turn the lights down and remind attendees to be silent. This helps them slip more easily into the willing suspension of disbelief. We seem to readily accept this policy for Broadway shows and films but not always for classroom reading. Obviously, we need light to read, so we can't turn off all the lights, but we need to realize that stiff chairs under fluorescent lights are not conducive to calm reflection and imagination.

Some kids and adults are pretty good at blocking out distractions and staying intensely focused on whatever task they are doing. More often, though, noises, doors opening and closing, people walking around the room, etc., will disturb someone trying to read, especially if that person is trying to *learn* to read. Disruptions knock the reader, as Nancie Atwell would say, "out of the zone." The classroom should have as few auditory and visual distractions as possible. Teachers need every minute available to create passion-readers.

One year, out of curiosity, Mr. Giorno and I calculated the class average for how many words a student could read per minute. The class average was 204. That figure provided a nice way for me to emphasize to the students how valuable every minute of independent reading was, and how disruptive every distraction was to our reading progress. Every minute we wasted because of nonsense meant 204 words we missed out on. It was an easy way to let them know that every minute counted and that we didn't want to squander any time with interruptions. There are many things that are beyond our control as teachers and parents, but if we are going to create passion-readers, we need to control the environment in which the reading is taking place.

We can improve lighting in the reading environment as well. Natural light and warmer artificial light work best. We need to set the stage for comfort in our classrooms. Whenever possible, turn off the overhead fluorescent lights and use lamps with warmer bulbs and natural light. I even use multicolored Christmas lights to bring warmth to the cold concrete walls of my classroom.

To really unwind and lose yourself in a text, you have to have more than one option for how to position your body. Sitting in a stiff chair all day does not help students to be relaxed and attentive. During independent reading time, it's important for kids to be able to get comfortable in whatever way suits their particular needs. When I am explicitly teaching concepts, my students face me and sit in a chair. Independent reading time is the perfect time for them to unwind with a book and curl up or stretch out wherever and however they choose—as long as they are reading. Some kids like to lie on the carpet, some like to prop themselves up against the wall with pillows, and some like to sit in their stiff chairs. A few big pillows with armrests and a sectional carpet provide a variety of options. As long as students are all locked-in and reading, it shouldn't matter where they sit.

Susan Cain accurately describes the "animal warmth" that comes from being in a group of people reading together, with each individual off on his or her own adventure of the mind. The kids love these periods of tranquility and introspection, and it is hard not to be moved when surveying a classroom of kids curled up reading their books together.

STRUGGLING READERS

Narrative immersion is structured around differentiated, personalized learning, so no matter how fluently a child reads—whether struggling or gifted—there is space for all to find success at their respective levels. There is no incentive for students to posture or feign superiority over their classmates. It takes peer competition out of the equation, because children are not measured in relation to their classmates—only themselves.

Kids who have struggled with reading sometimes feel frustrated and have a sense of failure. It helps them when the teacher takes the pressure off and shows pride in them when they have completed a book. It helps to remind students that every minute they spend reading, they are making themselves a little smarter. The kids who are struggling get it, and they are able to relax, pick a book they like that is at a comfortable level, and enjoy it as they practice reading more. They gradually make progress and feel satisfied with the accomplishment of reading as much as they have. They see firsthand how their practice has helped them. Struggling readers still need extra support from classroom teachers and reading specialists, but conducting your reading instruction like this will yield only positive results.

Audiobooks are enjoyable for all readers, but I find them especially helpful for struggling readers. Hearing a professional actor eloquently read the words in a way appropriate to the meaning and style of the text not only is entertaining but also models fluency, expression, and cadence. Following the text while listening to an audio version is beneficial for all students but especially so for students who struggle or have little experience being read to. How can children know what reading should sound like in their heads if they never hear it modeled aloud?

KINDLES + PROSODIC AUDIOBOOK NARRATION

Teaching in high-poverty environments presents specific challenges that can be very difficult to overcome. As Susan B. Neumann documents, the material disparity does translate into a print disparity, and building an extensive classroom library may not be not financially possible. There is a real need for an inexpensive method of bringing the daily experience of high-quality literature into high-poverty classrooms.

I teach in a neighborhood public school in a highly deprived area of North Philadelphia. Material resources are scarce, and many of my students are not enthusiastic about reading and read below grade level. Most of my students have experienced a wide variety of traumas associated with poverty and live with enormous stress.

Having a richly-stocked classroom library and pushing kids to read a large number of personally selected books is very effective, but many kids need unambiguously positive reading experiences before they have any desire to take a book off the shelf. Therefore, the more underperforming a class is, the more beneficial it is to shift your independent reading time toward audiobook time. I wanted to give disengaged students rewarding reading experiences to change their way of thinking about books, but I also needed a low-cost solution. Teaching reading with an emphasis on explicit skills instruction doesn't meet students' intrinsic motivational needs and and pretty much guarantees that many kids (especially those living in high-poverty neighborhoods) will dislike reading and therefore never practice it and never build the skills or background knowledge required to be a strong reader.

As a way of meeting these specific challenges, I purchased 30 Kindles (at $60 each), selected 30 excellent books, and bought 5 copies of each book (1 digital copy can go on 6 different Kindles), along with the 30 corresponding audiobooks. Assuming the Kindles are used each day for two separate classes of 30 students and the Kindles last for 3 years, the intervention costs only $20 per student.

Struggling readers often face the challenge that many books that appeal to their maturity level are too difficult for them to read, but with audiobooks they can follow along word for word in higher-level texts. By selecting books that are both well-written and high-interest, we can support the engagement of these students with books.

All students should be reading a variety of authors writing from diverse perspectives about diverse experiences. I intentionally selected 30 books covering a broad range of subjects. The books address physical disabilities, family issues, love, addiction, immigrant experiences, poverty, racism, resilience in the face of adversity, tough choices, celebrating life, and mortality. I want my students to read traditional classics like E.B. White's *Charlotte's Web*, as well as newer classics like Jason Reynolds's *Ghost*.

I bombard my students daily with high-interest, high-quality writing. I require them to track word-for-word on the Kindle as the narrator reads. I circle the room and help students who have lost their place. I stop by each student's desk repeatedly and he or she points silently with a finger to demonstrate successful tracking of the individual words along with the audio. I'll whisper some positive encouragement and then move on to the next student. The less students have been read aloud to, the more beneficial the audiobook modeling is.

Intensive reading practice and following along word-for-word with high-quality audio performances of the text provide students with abundant instructive modeling and improves their achievement levels. When you have a talented voice actor interpreting a text, some of the cognitive burden is lifted from the students and they can fall more easily into the natural rhythm of the text. Following the text during a read-aloud models all of the various intricate elements of prosody: pacing, pitch, volume, inflection, articulation, and pronunciation.

Classroom management can be extremely challenging, but if the right atmosphere is created and the story is strong enough, all students can focus and follow along on their Kindle as the actor reads. With talented voice actors reading audiobooks, students get the added bonus of hearing book characters' diversity reflected in the actors' voices; for example, in the way an African American female character is rendered by an African American female actor. When a rowdy classroom becomes silently engaged with an intrinsically captivating story, a serene focus ensues. Our most disengaged readers need this kind of aesthetic experience on a daily basis. We can see the intellectual results we seek by creating genuine engagement through a sustained, focused practice.

Dimming the fluorescent lights and relying instead on the warmth of table lamps and Christmas lights, I watch my students follow the text in their Kindles as the rich voice of an actor carries across the darkened room. The experience is comforting, engaging, communal, and therapeutic. The necessary conditions for profound reading experiences have been created. Regardless of each individual student's current reading ability, the whole class enjoys and shares the experience together. Combining the intensity of daily practice and high-interest, high-quality stories with prosodic narration is valuable instruction.

Audiobooks also build excitement for further reading. I remember one year, as soon as we finished listening to and reading along with the audiobook to *A Series of Unfortunate Events: The Bad Beginning* by Lemony Snicket, a student approached me and said, "This reminds me of my parents. They both died, and I've moved around to live with different relatives." When he told me that, it reminded me that the day before, he came in and told me he had done something wrong. He told me that he knew we were reading the book during class, but he couldn't help sneaking one of the class copies into his backpack and finishing the rest of the book that night. I told him I was glad he loved it and that he had nothing to apologize for. It's undoubtedly poignant that *A Series of Unfortunate Events*, with the over-the-top tragedy of the Baudelaire siblings, actually reminded a child of his own life, but by the time he had eventually torn through all thirteen books in the series, I think he might have dealt with some of his pain and experienced some positive growth by connecting with the siblings' story.

Art is a refuge, and reading can be a portable sanctuary. Schopenhauer writes that humans are in the unfortunate position of feeling pain but not painlessness. This predisposes us to fixate on our personal pain. When you read well-written stories, you can see the pain of others more clearly and realize that you are not alone, and this can ameliorate your loneliness. When you read about an ordeal suffered by characters in a story, you can be drawn in and enabled to share in their emotional journey. This phenomenon is why, when we follow the text as we listen to James Avery narrate Christopher Paul Curtis's *Bud, Not Buddy*, classes end with spontaneous applause.

A scarcity of positive reading experiences, a scarcity of appealing books, and a scarcity of reading practice hobbles our students. We need to ensure reflective dialogues—personal and collective—happen every day.

Narrative immersion can help fill in these formative gaps that especially affect children who live in poverty. No one wants to create tuned-out, test-taking automatons, but when we deny the needs of our students and neglect to create an authentic community in our classrooms—one defined by trust and support, that is exactly what we risk doing.

• • •

CHAPTER 4

INTENSIFYING INDEPENDENT READING TIME

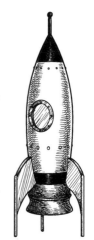

The best way to develop reading ability is to provide abundant opportunity for experiencing reading.

~ **RICHARD ALLINGTON**

Aristotle said *"Men become builders* by building houses, and harpists by playing the harp." And we become readers by reading. There are no shortcuts to excellence. If you are ever to become a first-rate reader, you quite simply need to read for thousands of hours. Thousands of hours of intentional practice is what builds mastery, and the best way to motivate such discipline is to make it enjoyable.

Schools deal with frequent disruptions and schedule changes, and unfortunately the changes typically come at the expense of the read-aloud and independent reading activities. In the past, I had only twenty minutes of independent reading time shoehorned into my daily schedule, and that just wasn't enough. It was also usually the first thing I cut when time was short. The message I was sending students was that reading a book that interests you is dispensable. But the message I wanted to be sending was the exact opposite—reading a book that interests you is not dispensable; it is *essential*. To send that message, I needed to elevate independent reading to be an essential part of the day.

It is clear that high-volume reading increases vocabulary and comprehension. In addition to English/Language Arts, Science and Social Studies rely on excellent reading skills. A strong vocabulary and high level of comprehension is also needed for any type of Math word problem. Additionally, we know that learning to write well is absolutely dependent on learning to read well. Every child I have ever taught who could write well was a voracious reader. The two skills are directly related, and strong reading habits are the prerequisite for strong writing skills. Cognitive scientist and linguist Steven Pinker explains:

> Language has a massive amount of irregularity: idiosyncrasies, idioms, figures of speech, and other historical accidents that you couldn't possibly deduce from rules, because often they are fundamentally illogical. The past tense of "bring" is "brought," but the past tense of "ring" is "rang," and the past tense of "blink" is "blinked." No rule allows you to predict that; you need raw exposure to the language. That's also true for many rules of punctuation. If I talk about "Pat's leg," it's "Pat-apostrophe-s." But If I talk about "its leg," I can't use apostrophe S; that would be illiterate. Why? Who knows? That's just the way English works. People who spell possessive "its" with an apostrophe are not being illogical; they're being too logical, while betraying the fact that they haven't paid close attention to details of the printed page.
>
> So being a good writer depends not just on having mastered the logical rules of combination but on having absorbed tens or hundreds of thousands of constructions and idioms and irregularities from the printed page. The first step to being a good writer is to be a good reader: to read a lot, and to savor and reverse-engineer good prose wherever you find it. That is, to read a passage of writing and think to yourself: "How did the writer achieve that effect? What was their trick?" And to

> *read a good sentence with a consciousness of what makes it so much fun*
> *to glide through.*

As he states, without this raw exposure to language through reading, you will not be able to write well. No amount of studying rules or practicing drills can make up the deficit. It's the equivalent of a brute-force attack in computer science. You spend a lot of time practicing the game, absorbing more and unlocking more with each repetition. When you learn to read, you slowly crack the code through extended practice, and the more you read, the less demanding and painful the process becomes, and thus the joy of reading begins to outweigh the tedium.

After we, as adults, have mastered the complexity of English, we develop a cognitive bias that makes it difficult for us to understand how confounding the process is from the student's perspective. The writer Luba Vangelova explains:

> *Adults who have already mastered written English tend to forget about its*
> *many quirks. But consider this: English has 205 ways to spell 44 sounds.*
> *And not only can the same sounds be represented in different ways, but the*
> *same letter or letter combinations can also correspond to different sounds.*
> *For example, "cat," "kangaroo," "chrome," and "queue" all start with the*
> *same sound, and "eight" and "ate" sound identical. Meanwhile, "it" doesn't*
> *sound like the first syllable of "item," for instance, and "cough" doesn't*
> *rhyme with either "enough," "through," "furlough" or "bough." Even some*
> *identically spelled words, such as "tear," can be pronounced differently and*
> *mean different things.*

If you want an excellent command of English, you cannot avoid practicing for thousands of hours. Only enjoyment can fuel this kind of discipline: without it, you will not be engaged and thus not follow through with the practice. So many students are tuned out of their education because it does not reward their efforts with anything plea-surable. They feel detached and alienated from the content, because it doesn't speak to their concerns. Ideally, children should have two hours every single day designated for independent reading.

BACKGROUND KNOWLEDGE, CULTURAL LITERACY, GROWTH MINDSETS, CRYSTALLIZED INTELLIGENCE, AND READING

I think sometimes in education we misunderstand intelligence. Social Psychologist Richard Nisbett provides some crucial insight on what we talk about when we talk about intelligence:

> *There are actually two components to g or general intelligence. One is fluid intelligence, or the ability to solve novel, abstract problems—the type requiring mental operations that make relatively little use of the real-world information you have been obtaining over your lifetime. Fluid intelligence is exercised via the operation of so-called executive functions. These include "working memory," "attentional control," and "inhibitory control." The information that you must sustain constantly in your mind in order to solve a problem, and that requires some effort to maintain, is said to be held in working memory. Attentional control is the ability not only to sustain attention to relevant aspects of the problem but also to shift attention when needed to solve the next step in the problem. And inhibitory control is the ability to suppress irrelevant but tempting moves.*
>
> *. . . The other type of general intelligence is called crystallized intel-ligence. This is the store of information that you have about the nature of the world and the learned procedures that help you to make inferences about it. The subtests on the WISC that tap crystallized intelligence most heavily are Information, Vocabulary, Comprehension, Similarities, and Arithmetic.*

> . . . *Simply convincing students that their intelligence is under their control to a substantial extent, can make a big difference in academic achievement.*
>
> . . . *IQ is only one component of intelligence. Practical intelligence and creative intelligence are not well assessed by IQ tests, and these types of intelligence add to the predictability of both academic achievement and occupational success. Once we have refined measures of these types of intelligence, we may find that they are as important as the analytic type of intelligence measured by IQ tests.*
>
> *Intelligence of whatever kind and however measured is only one predictor of academic and occupational success. Emotional skills and self-discipline and quite possibly other factors involving motivation and character are important for both.*

We can accomplish a great deal of what Richard Nisbett details in the development of intelligence by building crystallized intelligence through a very high volume of reading practice. Too often we label children with fluid intelligence "bright" and underestimate other children because we fail to recognize crystallized intelligence. Addressing this growth mindset approach is crucial to empowering our students. Students will bring various types of fluid intelligence to our classroom, and as teachers there isn't much we can do to affect them. And students will come with various types of crystallized intelligence, which we can affect enormously. When we boost students' crystallized intelligence, we push more of their cognitive load to their long-term memory. Thus, we free up their working memory to concentrate on comprehension and inference rather than semantic, syntactic, and graphophonic cues. In essence, we help students automatize the decoding process through thousands of hours of authentic practice, so that the process of decoding language becomes effortless and the mind's bandwidth is freed up for deeper comprehension.

We should not underestimate the value of background knowledge. In order to grasp new information, we need a solid base in which to connect this new knowledge. This schema cannot be imposed. It must be nurtured. By definition, a schema is created from the bottom up, yet we often speak as if the construction were from the top down. A student lacking a broad base of background knowledge and cultural literacy to make connections simply cannot absorb the same amount of information as one who does. We need to have a massive collection of books on a broad variety of topics in our classrooms for our kids to build that base and develop their crystallized intelligence.

EMBEDDING THE TIME

The best way to build sufficient time for independent reading and read-alouds into the curriculum is to keep it as simple as possible. The schedule below gives students the time they need to practice their independent reading but preserves flexibility, so that any school can adapt the sessions to their specific school idiosyncrasies.

Ideally a schedule should consist of:

- a daily 30-minute read-aloud session, first thing in the morning.

- 2 daily 30-minute independent-reading or audiobook sessions, whenever appropriate for your school's specific needs.

- 60 minutes of independent reading for homework or a 60-minute after-school club with audiobook support.

DIFFERENTIATED INSTRUCTION AND LEVELING

One of the most important benefits of teaching reading this way is that it enables highly differentiated instruction. Students can read texts at or near their individual levels. If a child is reading above grade level, he or she can be appropriately challenged. If a child is reading below grade level, he or she can be appropriately challenged as well. Because each student is working in that sweet spot just below his or her frustration level, all students can progress at their most effective rate. This is not to say they shouldn't be able to read easier or harder books, but mostly staying in their "zone of proximal development" is best. I love Nancie Atwell's terms "holiday book," "just-right book," and "challenge book." Atwell's approach gives students flexibility in their choices.

It can be tricky to monitor simultaneously all of your students' independent reading selections to determine if a student is reading too many counterproductive books, and, if so, to decide when to intervene. Typically, students self-adjust to the right difficulty level in their reading, abandoning a book that is too frustrating or quickly blowing through one that is too easy. I tend to trust the students and only intervene when I see a pattern that seems to be holding them back.

For example, I had a student who wanted to read exclusively manga, a type of Japanese graphic novel. He was a very reluctant reader and highly distractible, so I enthusiastically encouraged him to read in that genre as much as he wanted. After he had read about a dozen in a row, though, I decided it was time to nudge him in a new direction. Inspired by Donalyn Miller, I require each student to read several books in each of the major genres, so while it was good that he loved reading a certain kind of book, I knew it was time to broaden his horizons.

This is where the art of teaching comes into play. Good teachers intuitively sense when a student is confident enough for you to take off the training wheels and push him or her to the next level, whether that level is behavioral or academic. Throughout the day, teachers must constantly decide which battles to fight and which to let pass. An outside visitor might observe an isolated moment in a classroom and infer from students' behavior that discipline is lax. To the teacher, however, who has the needed background knowledge of the situation, the class will appear right on course.

For example, I had a student who struggled mightily with reading. He read word by word and it was clearly painful for him. Any assignment involving reading would take him three times longer than the average student, and his comprehension scores were extremely low. At the beginning of the year, he would pick books that were staggeringly difficult for him to read. He constantly looked away from his book during independent reading, and I could see that his text selection was not helping him and that he wasn't making progress. He was very self-conscious about his reading fluency, and it was perfectly understandable that he wanted to read the types of books the other kids were reading. I could tell that he had a sense of shame about his inability to keep pace with the others and that he would rather sit there for the whole session and fight with a book, however painful and useless that might be, than come across as a low-level reader to his peers.

Though reading was difficult for him, I noticed that during read-aloud time he listened intently and stayed engaged. He frequently comprehended things in the stories that other students missed. He loved to talk, he loved to sing, and he loved to tell entertaining stories. He loved spirituals, gospel music, and African American history. He had a big personality and a great sense of humor. Engaging with him during conferences and finding out what he cared about, I was able to coax him gently toward books more at his level and about things that mattered to him, without making him feel the least bit embarrassed.

He started reading books like *Henry's Freedom Box: A True Story from the Underground Railroad* by Ellen Levine and Kadir Nelson; Jeff Kinney's series *Diary of a Wimpy Kid*; and Doreen Rappaport and Shane W. Evans's books *Nobody Going to Turn Me 'Round: Stories and Songs of the Civil Rights Movement, Free at Last: Stories and Songs of Emancipation,* and the graphic novels *March: Book One* and *March: Book Two* about

John Lewis's life spent fighting for civil rights. By finding stories that spoke to him personally, he became free to discover directly the value of and the pleasure in reading. By December he told me: "This is the first time in my life that I actually like to read." Then he discovered the *I Survived* historical fiction series, which he proceeded to plow through one by one. What led to this result was immediate classroom access to high-interest books, the freedom to choose, a nonfrustrating level of reading, the daily time allocated to practice, and the proper guidance from a teacher. When those elements are in place, new passion-readers can emerge.

Differentiated instruction is not purely academic. Differentiated instruction applies to behavioral accommodation as well. To properly give each student what he or she needs, teachers must be flexible with some of the rules. For example, a student of mine once started the school year off in a bleak state of mind. His mother had recently passed away, he wasn't living where he wanted, and now he found himself back at his disfavored school. He was uncomfortable in our classroom, and avoided communication as much as possible. Something he nonverbally communicated to me, though, was the significance of his puffy jacket. This jacket appeared to be his armor. One of the rules at our school is that you have to take off your outerwear inside the classroom, but it was obvious to me that this jacket provided him with a great amount of comfort, so I bent the rules. This kid was doing everything I requested of him, but he had just one request for me—to let him wear this jacket in class. I drew the line on his hood being up during class, but when he was immersed and locked in reading Harry Potter, I'd see the hood up and let it pass. It may have looked unconventional to see a student during independent reading with his jacket on and hood up, but I was less concerned with the decorum of the situation than the fact that he was blasting through the Harry Potter series. It's impossible not to draw the conclusion that for this child, reading a series about a young boy coping with the death of his parents, living in a home not of his choosing, and then being shipped off to school in September had distinct personal relevance. Harry had his invisibility cloak, and my boy had his puffy jacket. It's harder to get more differentiated than that.

If you make a point at read-aloud time to explain to your students that people learn in different ways and at different paces and that there are multiple types of intelligence, you can help diminish the destructive connection between a numerical reading level and self-worth. A child should never feel shame about the books that are just right for them. Preventing this from happening can be tricky. You need to make sure a student reading at a higher level is not constantly coasting at a lower one when he or she really needs to be challenged. But what is low level for one student might be just right for another. The tricky part is making the judgment about what is appropriate for them individually so that you can coach them effectively. This is not to say that higher-level readers should never read books that are easy for them. It's good for them to have that flexibility as long as they are not shying away from more challenging fare.

As teachers, we have to deal with many circumstances that are out of our control. That makes it all the more important that we exercise the control we have to make small but enormously helpful accommodations such as allowing students to read books from various levels or wearing a special jacket during class. We need to deemphasize any competitiveness regarding reading levels and focus on children's personal needs. We should not encourage students to judge themselves by how many books they read in comparison with their classmates. It's not a conclusive race, but rather an experiential process. It's about students pushing themselves to their personal best. I want to make sure they fully apply themselves in an intentional intellectual practice. I want them to have the freedom to choose literature that is meaningful to them. I feel thrilled when a student finishes 60 or even 70 books and personally want to let them know how awesome an achievement that is. But since it is not a competition, I do not exalt them in front of the class. I am just as proud of the kid who consistently reads books that are just right for him (but could appear too easy for fifth grade) as the kid who reads a 700-page Harry Potter novel with his hood up.

With proper guidance, kids can understand that different students have different needs. You can offer this guidance by cultivating a classroom culture that disentangles learning and competition. Ranking kids according to a single narrow performance standard is antithetical to the nurturing of intrinsic motivation and authentic learning. When you decouple peer competition from your classroom instruction, kids can show remarkable understanding of each other's different needs.

Hemingway said, "There is nothing noble in being superior to your fellow man; true nobility is being superior to your former self." Empowering children to choose books they are interested in at their approximate level is the ultimate way to differentiate reading instruction. It teaches them not to define themselves based on how they measure up to someone else's performance but instead to become the best possible version of themselves.

• • •

CHAPTER 5

INSPIRING AUTONOMY THROUGH STRUCTURED CHOICE

"Is there any single word that could guide one's entire life?"
The Master said: "Should it not be reciprocity? What you
do not wish for yourself, do not do to others."

~ ANALECTS OF CONFUCIUS

Reciprocity is essentially humanity's golden rule, the mostly universally acknowledged, general social contract the world can agree upon. Yet we don't always give our students the dignity of reciprocity. Most adults would be outraged if they were forced to read books they weren't interested in. Chekhov wrote, "You must trust and believe in people or life becomes impossible." In many respects learning in schools becomes impossible, because of a lack of trust and belief in our students. Reading can inspire you to want to be a better person. It can enable you to enter reflective places and grapple with the big questions in your own life, questions no one else can answer but you. Escaping into these imaginative reading realms allows you to grab something ethereal and bring it back into concrete reality.

We should never confuse compliance with engagement. Our goal should not be creating what William Deresiewicz called "excellent sheep." We shouldn't be striving to produce compliant automatons, and we need to consider the child's experience of school as much as the child's performance in school. We need reciprocity; not permissiveness, nor uniform compliance, but structured choice.

You need other people to help you broaden your horizons, but you are the only person who knows the questions to which you long for answers. Teachers need to assist students in their discovery of their authentic selves. We should introduce students to as many new, stimulating books as possible, but they are the only ones who know what they are hungry for. Book conferences with a teacher are like check-up visits to a doctor. What's working, what's not, checking progress, etc. Much lip service is paid to differentiated instruction, but letting students choose books that are finely tuned to their personal interests is the ultimate in differentiated instruction. Doing so validates students as individuals, shows respect for their interests, and motivates them to become the best they can be.

I think there are intelligent choices that we can make to structure book selection in a way that both supports students' academic progress and preserves their freedom of choice. Taking a page from the science of behavioral economics, teachers need to curate their bookshelves to maximize academic utility. We do not have to choose between having students read only one particular book or letting them read whatever they want. We need a balanced menu to ensure students sample various genres but remain free to choose within those genres. Teachers need to select books for the class library that are both high-quality and high-interest, then leave students free to choose from among them. This gives students the best of both worlds. The teacher curates a vast, age-appropriate library that the student can freely explore and choose from.

Having structured choice encourages students to sample different genres, set firm goals, and push themselves to reach those goals. Behavioral economics tells us that having too many choices can be overwhelming and frequently leaves one feeling less satisfied, but a properly structured set of choices can encourage independence and creative experimentation. If choices are too open-ended and vague, the freedom to choose loses its power. Children need guidance and direction; without structure, they will be dizzy with freedom. The key is providing a rigorously structured system that encourages enjoyment and the exploration of personal interests in a way that promotes growth. Students need a predictable, structured routine that offers novelty and freedom.

We know that reading changes lives. So how do you make a child fall in love with reading? How do you make that quiet place of reflection and exploration not something confined to an English class but essential to the child's everyday life? Years ago, it occurred to me that if you wanted to turn the class from function-readers into passion-readers, a major intervention would need to take place. Inspired by people like Jim Trelease, Nancie Atwell, Donalyn Miller, Michael Smith, and Richard Allington, I decided to push as hard as I could to implement the kind of instruction I knew to be necessary.

REMEDIATING DISPARITY

Every man with a little leisure and enough money for railway
tickets, every man, indeed, who knows how to read, has it in his
power to magnify himself, to multiply the ways in which he exists,
to make his life full, significant and interesting.
~ ALDOUS HUXLEY

For obvious reasons, it is easier to become a passion-reader in an affluent home, than it is to do so in an underprivileged home. A major gap is the number of reading switches that affluent areas flip compared with underprivileged areas. Kids from affluent areas have a buffer which protects from certain types of issues. Underprivileged kids are consumed with stress about having their basic needs met, and they typically don't have the means to seek out underfunded libraries or virtually nonexistent bookstores. How can you be expected to know the power of deep reading if you've never been privy to its glory?

As Huxley suggests, if you have enough money and a little time, you can experience the transformative power of reading. But what if you have no disposable income, there are no interesting books at hand, and your school day doesn't provide the time? When your day-to-day existence is devoted to your physical survival and you are overwhelmed with stress concerning your basic needs, imagination is a luxury item.

While any programs that encourage family support are laudable and family support is welcomed and important, we cannot just outsource this responsibility to parents. The dramatic disparity between access to books in affluent areas and that in underprivileged ones needs to be addressed. This is a problem all schools must solve if we are to create a nation of engaged, reflective, and discerning citizens. Many kids from privileged backgrounds enjoy the encouragement of their parents and schools to pursue their passions and interests. But what about the kids who don't have that encouragement? How will they find opportunities to follow where their curiosity leads?

As it stands now, parents who are themselves passion-readers are most likely to attempt to raise children who are passion-readers. It takes an enormous amount of cultivation to raise a child who is a passion-reader. Most children raised in function-reader homes will not magically turn into passion-readers. The cultivation just isn't there to help such readers to grow. There are outliers, of course: the child that somehow finds his or her way to lifelong passion-reading thanks to a relative, librarian, or teacher flipping a switch or two, but they are the exception. If we take responsibility for flipping literacy switches in school, we can create not just outliers of passion-readers, but classrooms of passion-readers.

Good teaching needs balance: structure without rigidity, flexibility without permissiveness, discipline without cruelty, and praise with sincerity. Some schools find and maintain this balance, but many do not. We may hope that independent reading and read-alouds happen at home, but it only happens for the lucky ones. What about the kids to whom no one reads? What about the kids who don't receive support for independent reading at home? If you don't grow up with the modeling, the access to books, the time, and the quiet space, how would you even know what you are missing? Do we just shrug our shoulders in response to these kids? Or do we provide the necessary conditions for them at school?

The bottom line is that this intervention must take place at school. If it does happen at home, that is a wonderful bonus, but it's not enough to just hope anymore. For a passion-reader to be created at home, these stars must align:

- The child was raised appreciating the joy and power of being read to.

- There are books in the home.

- Those books are interesting to the child.

- Those books are relatively close to the child's reading level.

- If there are no books in the home, than that there is a sufficiently funded library in the neighborhood with open hours that suit a child's schedule.

- That there is an involved adult who has the free time or awareness to take them to a library.

- That their neighborhood is safe enough for the child to walk to the library.

- There is a quiet, comfortable space for them to read.

- There is an adult who models reading for the child.

- There is an adult who carves out time for the child to read.

Currently, we hope that the stars align and that all these variables out of our control tip in the right direction, and a reader is created. We need to do more than hope; we need to flip all the switches on in school and know we are helping create passion-readers.

I had a student many years ago whose life was barraged with tragic events. His only remaining family member was a very frail grandmother, who loved him dearly and did everything in her power to provide the best life for him. His neighborhood was dangerous, and he wasn't allowed outside. When his grandmother became bedridden, he played video games the entire weekend in the basement. He described to me his surprise when he would ascend from the basement, see daylight, and realize that he had played video games until the sun came up. As with him, so many children never have a chance to become lifelong readers, because they spend their time and energy dealing with overwhelming stress. For even the most well-meaning teachers, it's impossible to provide everything our children need. If we can succeed in making them literate, then we can improve their odds. Literacy can give children the means to save themselves.

That may seem a lot to ask of books, but reading does save lives. There are countless people that would attest to that. I have no doubt that if my student had passed his time in that basement reading instead of playing video games, he would have improved his shot at making it in the world. We have limited reach as teachers, but if we can make that reading magic happen in the short time we have in the classroom, we can change everything. We do have power over what transpires in those precious school hours, and we need to use that power. We need to assume that children won't have any literacy switches flipped, and, knowing how important first-rate literacy skills are, flip those switches for them.

Inspiring kids to become passion-readers takes more than flipping one switch in isolation. If you are going to create a passion-reader, you must address multiple components together. And it is not enough simply to talk up these components or encourage the children to implement them at home. We need to flip these in the only place we can control the environment: school.

LITERACY SWITCHES

1. 30 Minutes of Daily Read-Aloud

2. Immediate Access to High-Quality, High-Interest, Diverse Books

3. Distraction-Free Comfort

4. 2 Hours of Daily Independent Reading and Audiobook Support

5. Structured Choice

We can have high expectations of students while also preserving the joy of play, and not controlling every aspect of their play is essential. It is similar to how we support them by making sure the playground and equipment are safe and by monitoring and intervening when we see they need help. We must recognize that they need choice and freedom in their play to experience joy. We should check up on them periodically to make sure that they are progressing and that they get the extra support they need if they are not. When the school day, in contrast to the educational flow model, is incoherent and arbitrary, our kids become anxious. When the school day seems redundant and rigid, our kids become bored. Paradoxically, an obsession with children's immediate academic performance damages their long-term academic experience. Kids love play because it is a creative, self-motivated experience. Academic work needs to be creative and self-motivated as well. Being in a flow state can make it enjoyable. We recognize the flow state when kids play, and we need to support it when they read. Adding layer upon layer of Kafkaesque paperwork and consuming valuable time with constant measurement and meaningless tasks is like adding layer upon layer of paint—to the point that the paint obscures the object it covers. We need to scrape off several layers of paint in education, recalibrate, and get back to the fundamental roots of how we not only learn but also thrive.

The conclusion is inescapable that our kids need to read what they are intrinsically motivated to read about for literally thousands of hours to achieve a high level of reading comprehension. They need us to provide the guidance, time, and books. Denying children intellectual agency, as we already know, works against motivation and high-performance. Reading comprehension is the cornerstone of education. High performance in Science, Writing, Social Studies, and word problems in Math is impossible without superior comprehension. We need to prioritize helping children become passion-readers as the foundation of the curriculum.

THE SIGNIFICANCE OF READING ALOUD AND GIVING BOOK TALKS

Good picture books can be just as profound as books of philosophy. For example, the book *Malala, a Brave Girl from Pakistan/Iqbal, a Brave*

Boy from Pakistan: Two Stories of Bravery by Jeanette Winter is a sublime meditation on freedom and courage. When I read that book aloud, the class is held rapt by the delicate pictures and poetic language, but they are also stirred to ask themselves, "How could she be so brave? How could he be so brave? Could I be so brave? Would I be so brave?"

It is worth noting that reading aloud doesn't only benefit the kids. As a teacher, I find it reinvigorating to read about new books that are coming and to feel the excitement of sharing them with my students. Schools can support teachers in this endeavor by giving them opportunities in professional development and faculty meetings to discuss new book titles and by providing them funds to purchase copies. Reading aloud helps prevent teacher burnout by making each day novel and exciting, creating a state of flow for the teacher as well. When we don't capitalize on the power and joy of stories in education, we neglect not only our students' emotional and academic needs, but also our own as well. The combination of fresh new stories with the variety of the kids' personalities creates original, authentic conversations every day. And incorporating book talks during the read-aloud time in the morning makes the activity even more rewarding. When we are already gathered together to hear stories is the perfect time and place for the kids to share with the class. Additionally, book talks and read-alouds align perfectly with the speaking and listening strands of the Common Core State Standards.

BOOK TALK

- Show the book cover to the class.

- Tell us the title, author, and genre.

- Briefly introduce the main characters.

- Read the back of the book or a favorite passage from the book.

- Without spoiling any surprises, give a brief summary.

- Is it a holiday book, a just-right book, or a challenge book? Why?

- Explain why you love this book.

- If you love books about _____, then you would love this book too.

THE READER'S NOTEBOOK AND ACCOUNTABILITY

The pioneering work of Donalyn Miller and Nancie Atwell has been essential in developing the right format for our reading instruction. There needs to be a way for the children to set high, yet achievable, goals and to help them make steady progress toward those goals. If you do not provide the proper support or hold students accountable, they will not fulfill their potential. A great tool we have used for goal-setting, reflection, accountability, and conference preparation is Heinemann's *Reader's Notebook: Advanced*. We set the goal in the letter sent home over the summer that each child will read 40 books by June. We emphasize this during the first day of school in September, and at our back-to-school night for family members. All of our students and families are clearly aware of this 40-book goal and what it takes to reach it. To avoid giving students an incentive to read the shortest books possible, Donalyn Miller cleverly stipulates that extra-long books (around 400 pages) count as 2 books. That way we don't discourage our students from reading longer books.

The genre requirements can be adapted to suit your classroom's and school's particular needs. Maybe you need a little more historical fiction to satisfy your Social Studies curriculum requirements, or maybe there is a special emphasis at your school on Traditional Literature for your grade. All you would have to do is increase the genre you need and decrease another genre requirement. The important thing is that 40 books is ambitious but realistic, and if your students read a minimum of 40 books from a variety of genres—books that they are curious about and that they select—then they will be well on their way to becoming passion-readers.

Here are the Genre Requirements that we use for fifth grade:

7 Realistic Fiction

3 Historical Fiction

2 Traditional Literature (Folktales, Fables, Myths, Legends)

4 Fantasy

2 Science-Fiction

2 Biography/Autobiography/Memoir

3 Mystery

4 Informational Text/Nonfiction
5 Poetry
8 Hybrid/Genre-Free Choice
40 Books Total

INFORMAL CONFERENCING

We monitor our students' reading development through the Reader's Notebook. It is an excellent tool for tracking their independent reading progress throughout the school year. It is also a critical part of documenting their growth and gathering information. Every night for homework they read independently for 60 minutes and record an entry in their Reader's Notebook. I have my students choose a question from the "Suggestions for Writing About Reading" page that they find relevant and respond with at least five strong sentences. They choose which question to respond to each night but have to answer each question at least once before the end of the school year. Each time they answer a question, they simply place a checkmark next to it. Every morning I walk around the classroom, stop at their desks, silently read their Reader's Notebook response, and give them some quick feedback.

That response in the Reader's Notebook is the foundation for the daily informal conferencing that takes place when I stop by their desks to check their homework. Formative assessments like these are valuable, because checking in with each student every day, casually and informally, gives them immediate feedback and shows that you care about them. The relationships I build with my kids supersede any piece of paper or data point. Relationships matter, and the more time we spend building genuine relationships—and the less on paperwork—the better our pedagogy. Using formative assessment is the best way, not only to get up-to-the-minute information about students, but also to build genuine trust and respect. Formative assessment is immediate, direct, and powerful.

This is why formative assessment is so important. By giving students daily personal attention and feedback, you are helping them develop themselves as independent readers. You are also holding them accountable. After I read their Reader's Notebook responses, I speak with them informally right there at their desks. It doesn't have to be anything dramatic. I'm just checking in with their daily reading progress in an authentic way. These are a few of the comments I typically make:

- I see you started reading _____. How do you like it?

- _____ is reading this too; you two should talk about it.

- It seems that you really like _____ books. You might want to try _____ too.

- _____ just finished this book and loved it. Would you recommend it?

- How is this book? The cover looks really interesting.

The Reader's Notebook check helps me get to know them better as readers in small but frequent increments. I am paying attention to what they are reading and helping them make further connections to what other kids are reading, other authors they might like, and other series they might enjoy.

FORMAL CONFERENCING

The Reader's Notebook is also used in our more formal conferencing. Once a month, each student gets a one-on-one conference. The independent reading conference format I use is as follows: The students bring their Reader's Notebook and current independent reading book. If they just began a new one, they can bring a book they recently completed. I review the progress they are making with their 40-book goal and genre requirement. I highlight strengths or weaknesses and maybe point out some genres they have neglected. I use an independent reading conference form to ask them questions about their books and reading progress, and I record notes on the form.

As we review their progress toward their goals, and they see their list of completed books lengthen, the children experience the satisfaction of their achievement. This more formal one-on-one conferencing is an opportunity to develop a personal relationship with students and to get to know them better as individuals. Knowing that a particular student is crazy about reading animal books helps me make connections to other books she might like. She wants to be a veterinarian, so she tries to select books that would improve her knowledge of animals. Maybe she will be a veterinarian, and maybe she won't. But reading every single book with a dog on its cover and reading informational science books about animals are only going to make her a smarter person and a better reader, even if she decides not to pursue that career path.

Individual conferences offer a chance to make the time and space to be fully present to each child and to fully listen to him or her. It's a struggle for teachers to make time when they have so many obligations, and it's not reflected in any particular data point, but it's more important than any data point. It's worth making the time to connect with your students and develop the intangible but invaluable relationship that helps you both succeed. It's the things you can't count which matter the most. And the most valuable thing you can give someone is your time.

• • •

INDEPENDENT READING CONFERENCE

Name: _____ Date: _____

- Student brings Reader's Notebook and current independent reading book to the conference.

- Teacher reviews Reader's Notebook with student, checking progress toward the 40-book goal and the genre requirement.

- Teacher uses the following prompts and questions to record notes.

Title:

Author:

Genre:

This is a: Holiday Book _____
            Just-Right Book _____
            Challenge Book _____

What made you select this book?

Are you enjoying the book? Tell me about what you do or do not enjoy.

What is the book about?

Tell me about the setting.

Introduce the main characters to me.

What is your favorite part so far?

What do you predict will happen in the rest of the book?

Read a favorite passage to me.

When did you start this book, and when do you think you'll finish it?

What are your strengths as a reader?

What reading skills would you like to improve?

Where do you usually read on the weekend, and for how long?

What goals do you have as a reader?

Tell me your plan for reaching these goals.

CHAPTER 6

QUANTIFYING THE STUDENT EXPERIENCE

This is the most effective way: let the growing soul look at life with the question: "What have you truly loved? What has drawn you upward, mastered and blessed you?" Set up the things that you have honored in front of you. Maybe they will reveal, in their being and their order, a law which is fundamental of your own self. Compare these objects. Consider how one of them completes and broadens and transcends and explains another: how they form a ladder which all the time you have been climbing to find your true self. For your true self does not lie deeply hidden within you. It is an infinite height above you—at least, above what you commonly take to be yourself.

~ **FRIEDRICH NIETZSCHE**

B randon and Vicky came to me in fifth grade with their passion-reading engines already built. All they needed from me was the book fuel to keep it running, which I did my best to provide. In many ways, this endeavor has been about reverse engineering Brandon's and Vicky's passion-reading engines so we can build ones for other kids. I wanted to investigate their development as readers and learn what helped or hindered their achievement.

BRANDON

Brandon was a new student in fifth grade, and it was immediately apparent that he liked to read. That particular year we split the classes by gender, and I was assigned the boys: eighteen of them obsessed with football and making jokes. It was a lot of fun, but out of a class full of witty, intelligent kids, Brandon seemed to be the only one who actually enjoyed reading. After he graduated from our elementary school, we kept in touch and continued to talk about reading and books. Brandon continued to excel throughout school and had his pick of universities. Brandon decided on Harvard, and when I found out he won a Gates Millennium Scholarship, I was curious to read the essay he had submitted. Here is his essay:

Love of Books Leads to Academic Success

For some reason, my classmates do not believe me when I answer the question: "How did you get smart?" by pointing to the long list of books I have read since I began devouring them sometime around second grade. They give me incredulous glances and sneer at the concept of "simple reading" being the key to academic success. It truly is a shame they do not believe me, because after truly examining my intellectual growth throughout the past twelve years, I accredit more than 50 percent of my knowledge to what I gleaned while reading a book.

For the record, I do not read textbooks, or encyclopedias, or dictionaries. I am a lover of fiction, and a purveyor of fantasy, and I have recently taken to dubbing myself a "dabbler" in science fiction. More often than not, I am reading about things that have never happened in all of humanity's history. I read about things taken right out of the vivid imagination of the author, stuff that wouldn't hold up against the harsh, fact-based reality of the world. I have not learned a myriad of specific, physical skills from reading, because very few writers go into excruciating detail when describing simple processes like changing a tire, or knotting a tie. But I have acquired a few specific skills that have acted as gateways into the world of other knowledge I have obtained.

Curiosity.

The answer lies between a book's pages. More often than not, I have no idea what some writers are talking about. There are authors (like Donna Tartt) who manage to employ beautiful strings of advanced vocabulary throughout their novels. I know a lot of words, but I am not a walking human dictionary, nor can I automatically derive the hidden connotations of every word that I come across. In order to be an avid reader and actually get something out of it, I had to acquire the skill of relentless curiosity in the very beginning. With it, the world became open. Topics and themes that would normally soar over my head became things that pinged my attention and sent me scrambling to the internet to discover the meaning. When I heard of new scientific theories, I would barrage the budding scientists in my life with endless questions to better understand exactly what the authors would talk about.

And while I have found knowledge in many other places besides books, literature has been the one constant "school" in my life. I never have to ask for permission to enter the pages of a novel and discover something new about the world around me. I have learned more about the human condition and the manner in which humanity carries itself through reading than any introductory psychology course at my high school could have taught me.

I have connected to a central hub of sorts through literature—the depository where authors dump fragments of their personal experiences and observations of the people around them. Because of literature, I have developed not only curiosity, but the keen ability to understand and to empathize with the people around me. There are very few emotions that I have not experienced transitively through the conduit of a novel, and because of that vast internalized understanding of human emotions, I have been able to expand upon my interpersonal skills.

Because of reading, and because of literature, I have developed a host of intangible skills, things I cannot demonstrate with my body, only with my character. Leadership, although it has been undoubtedly tempered by experiences at school, grew out of my love affair with tales of heroism in novels. It was a skill that I revered, and one I truly wanted to emulate. Reading tales of people leading their teams, their units, and their families throughout life gave me perspective on leadership before I even had the chance to actively practice it. It is perhaps because I got to watch (or rather, read) various styles of leadership in action at a young age that I was able to jump so readily into leadership as a teenager.

Perhaps the most important intangible skill I derived from my ravenous reading exploits is my sense of morality. Good and evil sit in the center of every good story. Sometimes it is obvious which side is which. The good guys often brandish gleaming swords of righteousness and are from the beginning of the story slated against the proverbial "dark witch." But there are also stories where good is indistinguishable from bad, where the bad guys wear the same smiles as the good guys; where each side is motivated by something that they believe to be inherently "good."

More than anything, these novels have taught me about the multiplicity of morality—how ambiguous and overall ill-fitting the terms "good" and "evil" are. In the world, there is no definite right and wrong because everyone looks at the world from a different perspective. Reading so many stories that have accentuated this fact has given me the cognizance necessary to understand the intrinsic motivations behind people's actions, and also develop my own understanding of what is and is not "moral."

In many ways, the true Renaissance man is not he who studies the physical crafts in school, or learns them through apprenticeship. Knowledge of the deeper, more everlasting kind can be learned simply from picking up a book and appreciating it for the lessons within. I have not physically experienced a lot of things in my life, but my mind has been places my body has never been—learned things that my hands will never understand. Foraging *through the pages of the many novels I have read throughout my life, has been my way of obtaining knowledge and I value the intangible skills I have developed more than I do any tangible skills I have learned elsewhere.*

After I read Brandon's profound essay, I was reminded of a passage in Richard Nisbett's book *Intelligence and How to Get It*. The synchronicity is striking.

Genes as Triggers of Environmental Influences
~ RICHARD NISBETT

Developmental psychologists Sandra Scarr and Kathleen McCartney, as well as economist William Dickens and philosopher and IQ scientist James Flynn, propose a further reason why the role of genes is overestimated. Slight genetic advantages can be parlayed into great IQ advantages because of the way they influence the kinds of experiences an individual has. Consider a basketball analogy. The child who is somewhat taller than average is more likely to play basketball, more likely to enjoy the game, more likely to play a lot, more likely to get noticed by coaches and encouraged to play for a team, and so on. That height advantage is totally dependent on such environmental events for its expression. And identical twins reared apart are likely to have very similar basketball experiences, because they are of similar height, so they are likely to end up with similar skills in basketball. But their similarity in basketball skills is not due to their possessing identical "basketball-playing genes." Instead it is due to genetic identity in a narrower attribute that causes them to have highly similar basketball-related experiences.

A similar point can be made about intelligence. A child with a relatively small genetic advantage in, say, curiosity is more likely to be encouraged by parents and teachers to pursue intellectual goals, more likely to find intellectual activity rewarding, and more likely to study and engage in other mental exercises. This will make the child smarter than a child with less of a genetic advantage—but the genetic advantage can be very slight and can produce its effects by virtue of triggering environmental "multipliers," which are crucial for realizing that advantage. All of this gene-environment interaction (or as geneticists would prefer to say, gene-environment correlation), however, gets credited to heritability, given the way heritability is calculated. This is not wrong, but it leads to an underestimation of the role of the environment.

To make it even clearer why heritability estimates slight the role of the environment, let's return to the basketball analogy. Suppose a child of average height is encouraged to play basketball, perhaps because her older siblings are players and keep a well-used hoop on the driveway. And suppose another child, of above-average height, has little access to basketball experiences, perhaps because she lives in a rural area and there are no neighborhood kids nearby. The taller child from a rural area is not likely to become much of a basketball player, whereas the average-height child has a reasonable chance of becoming good. Now we have a child with a genetic disadvantage who nevertheless is pretty good at it. Genes count, and given a constant environment they may have a big influence in determining talent. But environmental interventions can greatly influence— even largely override the effects of genes. This is particularly important for estimates of the effects of the environment on IQ. It is easy to imagine any number of ways in which intellectual pursuits can be made more or less available and attractive.

Narrative immersion is about making intellectual pursuits more available and more attractive. Currently we are not successfully creating the school environment necessary to cultivate readers. To bake a cake, you need to follow the right directions for combining ingredients. At school, every child comes to us with a different mix of ingredients, and we try to use the same directions to bake the same cake. We should be trying to find the right directions for the specific ingredients.

In an attempt to analyze what led to the passion-reading switch within Brandon, I had a conversation with him in which I asked him to recollect his formative reading experiences and to identify what he felt made the difference in his success.

A CONVERSATION WITH BRANDON

Well, when I was in first grade my teacher had us read outside of our required reading. She had a reading competition format, and we were trying to read as many books as possible, and she had a full library, and she would always let us go to the different floors in the building and borrow books from other people. She made it a point for us to read outside of our normal curriculum.

Harry Potter was definitely the first experience where I really enjoyed reading. My mom said she remembers coming into my room at nighttime and turning off my light and grabbing the book, because I used to go to sleep with it right on the front of my face. Every afternoon I just sat down and read all the way through it. And honestly, the first time I read Harry Potter I probably didn't understand any of it, but it was just the fact that I was able to get through such a big book. I think that was the first thing that said, you know what? This might be something you want to keep doing.

My favorite authors right now are Neil Gaiman and Donna Tartt, and I really got into Donna Tartt last year when I read The Goldfinch, and she has a really particular way with language. It's so beautiful. It's like one of those endless run-on sentences, but it makes sense at the end. Not everyone can accomplish something like that, and so I started reading through her novels. And Neil Gaiman is just a beautiful story teller. I never read short stories before and liked them, but I read some of his short story collections and now I'm addicted to them.

I don't do a lot of reflection after every single novel, but I think I absorb pieces from every novel along the way. Because I'll read a book and go through the characters' experiences and think of something similar in my life, or is this a way that I could handle something. I don't think it's been one book that influenced me the most. It's been the cumulative experience of reading books that has crafted me into the person I am today.

A couple of people encouraged me to love reading. Definitely you, because you gave me a ton of books when I was in fifth grade, and I still have that one big book you gave me, The New York Times Guide to Essential Knowledge: A Desk Reference for the Curious Mind. *In seventh grade, our classroom was stocked with books, and we did the Scholastic book orders, so I always had something new to read. And Ms. Bigelow in high school. It's one thing to read for pleasure and another thing to read on an academic level, and she sort of blurred those two lines together because she made me realize that once you read a certain amount of books for pleasure, it's important for you to look back at the ones that everyone says you need to read, the classics, because then you start to understand everything else better. So, she pushed me into the classics and the craft of writing.*

I probably became a strong reader in ninth grade, because that was the first time I had a job and I could buy books, instead of just borrowing them from the library. So, when you go to Barnes and Noble, and you're just perusing around, you come into contact with a lot of books that you otherwise would never have the opportunity to come into contact with. You learn a lot from them, and then it makes you want to keep reading. And I think the volume of books that I read between ninth and tenth grade really made me a stronger reader than ever before, because I was reading things that were beyond my grade level, beyond my plane of thinking, and it was pushing me to become better. So that's probably the time that I became the strongest.

There are two major things that I enjoy about reading. One is the imagination behind it, because it's an impressive feat to put together an entire story and be able to craft a million different characters, and someone I admire for being able to do that is George R.R. Martin, from Game of Thrones. *He has like thousands of characters, and somehow he keeps*

> it all together. I love all the imagination, and that's why I lean toward
> fantasy and fiction, more than any other genre. The second thing I really
> enjoy about reading is the craft, and I watch how other people make their
> sentences and novels and develop their characters. Because I've had the AP
> English experience the last couple years, I'm sort of honing in on those cer-
> tain elements, and it's fun to see how people have evolved and manipulate
> language. It's exciting to see books that can do that.

What Brandon says is very similar to what Nietzsche has to say
about the seriousness of craft. When we focus too much on the "daz-
zling whole," we can misattribute the finished product to purely innate
talent, and neglect to see the enormous time and diligence that went
into honing the craft.

THE SERIOUSNESS OF CRAFT

> Speak not of gifts, or innate talents! One can name all kinds of great men
> who were not very gifted. But they acquired greatness, became "geniuses"
> (as we say) through qualities about whose lack no man aware of them likes
> to speak; all of them had that diligent seriousness of a craftsman, learning
> first to form the parts perfectly before daring to make a great whole. They
> took time for it, because they had more pleasure in making well something
> little or less important, than in the effect of a dazzling whole. For example,
> it is easy to prescribe how to become a good short story writer, but to do
> it presumes qualities which are habitually overlooked when one says, "I
> don't have enough talent." Let a person make a hundred or more drafts of
> short stories, none longer than two pages, yet each of a clarity such that
> each word in it is necessary; let him write down anecdotes each day until he
> learns how to find their most concise, effective form; let him be inexhaust-
> ible in collecting and depicting human types and characters; let him above
> all tell tales as often as possible, and listen to tales, with a sharp eye and

ear for the effect on the audience; let him travel like a landscape painter
and costume designer; let him excerpt from the various sciences everything
that has an artistic effect if well portrayed; finally, let him contemplate
the motives for human behavior, and disdain no hint of information about
them, and be a collector of such things day and night. In this diverse exer-
cise, let some ten years pass: and then what is created in the workshop may
also be brought before the public eye.

But how do most people do it? They begin not with the part but with the
whole. Perhaps they once make a good choice, excite notice, and thereafter
make ever worse choices for good, natural reasons.

Sometimes when reason and character are lacking to plan this kind of
artistic life, fate and necessity take over their function, and lead the future
master step by step through all the requisites of his craft.

At this point in our conversation, Brandon and I went on a long digression about *Game of Thrones* and developing substantial emotional attachments to fictional characters. I mentioned a favorite quote of mine from George R.R. Martin: "A reader lives a thousand lives before he dies. The man who never reads lives only one." And our discussion turned to how we felt our lives are so much the better because of the thousand lives we've been able to live through literature. We both felt reading helps one live a richer, more complete life. We discussed how one understands people's motivations better and connects with people on a deeper level if one is a passion-reader, precisely because that person has had the experience of walking in all these different worlds. Brandon then turned the conversation to how these imaginative mental reading experiences translate into real-world benefits.

I think that's what sort of pushes me. I want to get into politics, and people
ask me: "Well, Brandon, why are you interested in politics of all things?"
And I think what sort of pushed me in that direction was being able to

experience vicariously through books how people live, and understand that there are different ways of living, and there are different options for living, and if I can sort of integrate all that into some sort of policy that could make somebody's life better, than that's perfect. I'll have this background knowledge from the millions of books that I'll try to read. And I think more than anything else, more than student council or anything, being able to experience the lives of characters through books has given me the knowledge I need to become a politician.

I think being able to read, aside from whatever somebody is assigning you, actually makes you more likely to actually get through the books that are being assigned to you. So as a student in a literature class, of course you are going to do well, but you get information that helps you in all other facets of your academic life. Like history: I never liked history when I was in elementary school, but once I was in high school, I was able to read some of the other books that intertwined history into the fantasy and fiction that I was reading, which made me more interested in what I was learning in class. I think the energy that somebody puts toward pleasure reading directly translates into improving their academic life.

Reading definitely led me to Harvard. I tell people that all the time, and I was just lecturing the kids in the high school, that they needed to be reading just as frequently as I did because it makes you a better academic, and it makes you think about the world around you more critically. It takes a lot to get into Harvard, and it takes a lot to write the college admissions essays that you need. And in order to get the best ones you have to be able to pull from experiences that you weren't always able to have, but there are experiences that you may have gotten from books. That's what I did with a lot of my college essays, and I think that's what sort of put them over the top and got me into the different colleges. Reading definitely got me into college, and it definitely made me into the leader that I am today, because I was able to experience through different characters how they handled leadership positions and *how they handled different situations. And it has influenced the way I've handled things.*

It's especially important for students to have control over their book selection. A lot of people look at classics and they say, "Well, people need to read these specific books because they have the themes that evolve through this genre, and the classics are the original source of these themes." And that's all well and good, but as long as the books have the themes, the kids are still learning what they need to learn. So, if teachers can sort of find books that kids will relate to, that have the same themes as the classics have, then they will be learning what they need to learn anyway, and learning in a pleasurable environment. Then later on, they will want to go back and look at the classics, because they will under-stand what has evolved from them, and they will be more eager to go back and look at the source. But in the beginning there needs to be plea-sure reading, so they can find out the information in the different genres the way they want to find it out, or else they won't want to read at all. And that's what you see with a lot of high school students now; they are handed down books from ages ago, and they don't want to read through the dense language of it. They would much rather read something that is relevant to them.

There are so many different things in a book that can relate to your own life, and so there is no reason to not pick up a book, and go through that flight simulator and be able to look at how a different character handled the situation. And since people love video games so much, it's sort of like being in a video game and having two lives. The first life is through the book and you get to sort of feel your way around and make mistakes, and then in your actual life, because you've experienced how a character made those mis-takes in the book, you can actually act in a more responsible and intelligent way. So, I would say if you don't read for the sake of pleasure, then read for the sake of being able to go further in life, because that's what it's going to be doing for you.

VICKY

Vicky is another passion-reader who was a past student of mine in fifth grade. Like Brandon, she came to fifth grade with her passion-reading engine already built. I spoke with her as she was finishing eighth grade. I wanted to reverse-engineer her engine, and see what we could learn from it. I asked Vicky to write an essay describing her personal thoughts about reading. This is what she sent me:

The Reading Experience

The reading experience is the amazing process in which a reader is unknowingly changed by what he or she has read over a period of time. These changes lead readers toward uncovering those hidden parts of themselves that are trapped between those pages and are waiting to be unleashed. Limiting readers'—or in this case, students'—choices, however, would mean limiting what parts of themselves they can discover, and that is just not fair. Not limiting a student's choices when it comes to reading allows them to undergo the full, uncut "reading experience."

The reading experience starts the moment a person decides to pick up a book and starts to get into it. The next thing they know, they have begun to develop a connection with the characters and have become slightly obsessed with the story's plot. The reader has then unknowingly become addicted to the story, and that I believe is the fascinating part of the whole thing, the fact all of these changes occur without your knowledge. Reading also works wonders for the mind and the spirit. It allows one to truly understand things, look at things differently, and lets one's imagination run wild! Most people underestimate the power of a good book. It's more than just a bunch of flimsy papers bound together by a spine. It's a journey—an escape. It is so much more than it appears to be. I could say more, but I'd be straying too far from my point: students should be able to choose what they can read for school.

I'll use myself as an example. I'll be honest, I was (and kind of still am) the awkward one among my classmates, so books were pretty much all I had. I was fine with the reading material that was assigned to us, but the books I picked out on my own were, hands down, my favorite. Going back to this concept of the reading experience, it really starts when you can deeply relate to some of the characters in the stories you read. I remember being younger and never being seen without a book in my hand. I also remember feeling like the characters I came across were my true friends because they understood me. It was and still is a great feeling to be truly understood, especially when you are surrounded by people who think they get you—like really get you—but don't. As kids, that's all we want—to be understood while we are trying to understand ourselves. Allowing kids to choose what material should be assigned to them at school would not only benefit us mentally, but also academically since there is a much greater chance of us understanding what is being taught while we are also getting a better understanding of ourselves.

I remember reading The Diary of Anne Frank on my own, and I was at the point in the story when she had an epiphany. Anne realized she didn't want to be a movie star or an actress anymore; she just wanted to be a writer. She learned that she, herself, was her biggest critic because she knew what sounded good along with what did not. It's crazy, because at the time I read it, I did not know why that seemingly simple statement resonated so deeply with me, but now I know. I want to write. Maybe not as a job . . . I don't really know yet. It's just something in the way it makes me feel. This situation in particular brings me to my next point: Reading allows one to both discover and develop the different parts of oneself. The "self" is very complex. There's your athletic self, your artistic self, and your various other "selves." But, in this case, I am actually referring to my literary self. The parts of the self that are affected depend on what genres you are into. For example, if you are reading a romance novel, that's your romantic self. Or reading a murder mystery novel, that is your investigative self. Therefore, limiting students' choices when it comes to reading is the equivalent of limiting what parts of themselves they can discover—and that just does not make sense. School is the place where you develop and discover yourself as a whole, so limiting students' literary choices means this purpose of developing and discovering yourself is not being fulfilled.

When it comes to reading, student choice allows the students to undergo the full, uncut "reading experience." This experience begins the moment he or she picks up a book and gets very interested in it. This interest is then spiked when the reader deeply connects with the characters they come across, which leads them to discover those hidden parts of themselves and develop those parts. These changes push the reader to be unknowingly changed in the best way—by unleashing a whole new understanding and perspective that will allow the student to benefit both mentally and academically.

I think these essays quickly demonstrate how fortunate I have been to teach such complex and brilliant students. Vicky's essay reminded me of something else Nietzsche wrote in *Human, All Too Human*:

Worshipping the Genius Out of Vanity

Because we think well of ourselves, but in no way expect that we could ever make the sketch to a painting by Raphael or a scene like one in a play by Shakespeare, we convince ourselves that the ability to do so is quite excessively wonderful, a quite uncommon accident, or, if we still have a religious sensibility, a grace from above. Thus our vanity, our self-love, furthers the worship of the genius, for it does not hurt only if we think of it as very remote from ourselves, as a miracle (even Goethe, who was without envy, called Shakespeare his "star of the furthest height," recalling to us that line "one does not covet the stars").

> But those insinuations of our vanity aside, the activity of genius seems
> in no way fundamentally different from the activity of a mechanical inven-
> tor, a scholar of astronomy or history, a master tactician. All these activi-
> ties are explained when one imagines men whose thinking is active in one
> particular direction; who use everything to that end; who always observe
> eagerly their inner life and that of other people; who see models, stimulation
> everywhere; who do not tire of rearranging their material.
>
> The genius, too, does nothing other than first learn to place stones, then
> to build, always seeking material, always forming and reforming it. Every
> human activity is amazingly complicated, not only that of the genius: but
> none is a "miracle."
>
> From where, then, the belief that there is genius only in the artist, orator,
> or philosopher? That only they have "intuition" (thus attributing to them
> a kind of magical eye glass by which they can see directly into "being")? It
> is evident that men speak of genius only where they find the effects of the
> great intellect most agreeable to and, on the other hand, where they do not
> want to feel envy. To call someone "divine" means "here we do not have to
> compete." Furthermore, everything that is complete and perfect is admired;
> everything evolved is underestimated. Now, no one can see in an artist's
> work how it evolved: that is its advantage, for wherever we can see the evo-
> lution we grow somewhat cooler.
>
> The complete art of representation wards off all thought of its evolution;
> it tyrannizes as present perfection. Therefore, representative artists espe-
> cially are credited with genius, but not as scientific men. In truth, to esteem
> the former and underestimate the latter is only a childish use of reason.

When we demystify "genius," we realize that we, too, are capable of
great things. Great achievements are not spontaneous, but result from a
grinding, focused concentration. We are too frequently presented with
the final, glossy product, and not the inconsistency, the toil, the false
steps which are all necessary to achieve it. What Brandon and Vicky have

accomplished is not luck. They have accumulated enormous amounts of "crystallized intelligence" through thousands of hours of reading. They have pushed through the sometimes frustrating, thorny process of literacy, because their curiosity pulled them.

As Nietzsche writes, "everything that is complete and perfect is admired; everything evolved is underestimated." When we simply admire the perfect, instead of understanding its evolution, we feel removed and incapable of great things. Print, as a medium, is uniquely suited to give us a glimpse into the insecurity, struggle, and conflict inherent in the achievement of great things. Other forms of media are typically more biased toward presenting fully complete, end products. Demystifying greatness can serve very real academic purposes, and is very much connected with cultivating a growth mindset.

When we admire people, we should be exploring how they accomplished what they accomplished—analyzing their path toward achievement. Reading is the perfect vehicle for this analysis. We should be observing the models that we admire and scientifically analyzing them. Instead of distancing ourselves from greatness, when we as readers comprehend this banality of high-achievement, we realize that we, too, can accomplish our own great things if we only apply the extraordinary time and effort. Reading hundreds of books is a way to discover this truth, and every book we read is a rung up the ladder toward our better selves.

A CONVERSATION WITH VICKY

I basically have liked to read since I started school. Like whenever I picked up a book, I would get into it, and it was basically like watching a movie in your head. From first through fifth grade I always had teachers read to me, and read-aloud time was always cool. I remember when our librarian used to read to us and do the voices and all that, and that was really cool.

I will get a little indecisive at times, and I don't know what books to read, so I like to get recommendations from people.

The first experience where I remember really enjoying reading was being in your class, and you were reading to us, and I could clearly depict what was going on, and I just found that really cool and I could get into it, just like the image part.

There are really too many favorite books to list. I'm reading Leaves of Grass, *and I'm halfway through* Song of Myself *right now, and, so far, it's really good. I'm not sure if I'm remembering the line precisely, but he was talking about how he sits content, and he doesn't really care what everybody else thinks.*

[I exist as I am, that is enough,
If no other in the world be aware I sit content,
And if each and all be aware I sit content.
One world is aware, and by far the largest to me, and that is myself,
And whether I come to my own today or in ten thousand or ten million years,
I can cheerfully take it now, or with equal cheerfulness, I can wait.
~ WALT WHITMAN]

I've been recently reading some John Green, and I like how he writes the story. He has his thoughts as he goes along, and he has his whole thought process in his books. And Americanah *[by Chimamanda Ngozi Adichie] related to me, because I'm Nigerian and I sort of know how that feels when people always feel the need to assume that they have this picture of how Africa is primitive, but it's not even really like that. It's like America, just a little more traditional. And reading* Americanah *made me think that, unlike Adichie, I have had to experience this double standard of being an American-born African. There is pressure on me to be knowledgeable about both American and African customs. And once you get* too into one side, you get accused of being a fraud and/or not embracing your culture.

The books that have influenced me most as a person, I don't remember precise titles, but nonfiction books help expand your imagination. You see how other people think and how out of this world it is. It's really cool. I like that.

My parents encouraged me to read. There was a point in time that I always carried around a book—like all the time—and they would see me reading and say, "You really like reading, don't you?," and my mom said "That's pretty good because it makes you smart." And I remember on Friday I was on the bus and the bus wasn't running, so I pulled out a book. And Omotara was sitting there talking to me, and she said, "You still love to read?" and I said "Yeah." And she said, "You know, that's really good for you." and I nodded and said "Yeah." And then Omotara said, "You're really smart, right? What's your GPA?" And I was like "4.0," and she said "Exactly!" And I was just sitting there thinking about it. And, of course, you encouraged me to read. Because you exposed me to all these different books and different genres, so that was cool. To be honest, a lot of this happened in fifth grade with you, because you were that avid reader. So when you sat there and read all these different books to us that talked about different things, like Bud, Not Buddy and Leaves of Grass, and there was the philosophy book by Lao Tzu [the Tao Te Ching].

I like how when you read a book there are times that you make connections that go on with your situation or with other books. Say, for instance, one Robert Frost poem that I read, "Hyla Brook." It was the last line that said, "We love the things we love for what they are." And I thought that was true, and the John Green book Paper Towns, the main character Quentin Jacobsen loved this girl named Margo Roth Spiegelman, but he realized that he loved this idea of her, not the real her. He liked her, but he didn't really know her—just the idea of her. So, I love making these contrasting connections in literature. It just helps develop your opinions on certain topics by recognizing alternative ideas—if that makes sense.

Reading changes my outlook on how I look at stuff. I can see something and see there's potential in it. Say there was this one time last month for national poetry month, when we had to pick an object in nature and write a poem about it. I wrote a poem about a dead tree, and, basically, I was talking about how there was potential in it, and how this tree is going to be really big one day.

I think reading for pleasure made me a stronger student because it's not something your teacher is forcing you to do, and it's not some little boring book that you have to read. Pleasure reading is for you. It means more because you love it. Kids should have control over book selection. If you pick it, then you're going to have to read it because you picked it. It makes sense. There's a greater chance of them reading, instead of giving them a boring book about the 1800s, or about the California Gold Rush, or something boring.

Reading will help you think in ways that you never thought you could think before. It will help you feel things that you never thought you could feel. And you can feel like you have a personal relationship with the characters.

Reading has led me to realize that I'm going to do something good one day. Do something big or great. And I don't know what it is yet, but I'm going to do something big. As long as I continue to read, I'll figure it out.

Brandon and Vicky are academic exemplars, and it's illuminating to analyze their growth into such excellent students and people. I don't want to take anything away from Brandon and Vicky—they are exceptional kids. But here's the thing. Most of the kids I teach are exceptional in their own highly specific ways. We need to help all of our children recognize whom they admire and what draws them upward and then fully support them in developing their highly specific personalities to the utmost. When we demystify mastery and view it instead as a fluctuating gradual evolution, we start to see—as Vicky saw in the tree—great potential.

Reading literature requires an examination of characters' insecurities, flaws, mistakes, self-doubt, and setbacks—and helps us realize that greatness isn't just innate talent bestowed upon certain lucky individuals. We realize that greatness in any endeavor is achieved through the gradual accumulation of knowledge and intentional rehearsal, and that we, too, are capable of greatness in our own highly specific ways. Reading is uniquely suited to facilitating this discovery, because readers are privy to the doubts, struggles, and internal monologues of characters' lives. Voluminous reading gives one a repertoire of complex experience, and guides one through the knotty work of synthesizing what one reads with what one has personally experienced.

When we don't allow students the breadth and freedom of choice that narrative immersion calls for, we are denying the intricate complexity of each child and the meaning he or she is desperately seeking to construct. Many kids don't like school because they find it irrelevant. Schools don't assist them in answering the highly specific questions they have. The key is to help them make academic progress by teaching them how to find answers to their questions. Make the school day more about what they find relevant by giving them choice. Reconfigure priorities in the classroom, so that students see learning as a journey to discover themselves and the world, rather than as a form of kidnapping and being held hostage to the mastery of irrelevant content.

Brandon and Vicky are both pursuing what lifts them upward. And not only is this leading them to become more complete people; but it is also academically enriching. It seems to me that Brandon and Vicky were born naturally more curious than others, and their stronger curiosity made them more quickly open themselves up to reading. Being born with an exceptional curiosity streak made them pursue reading more, which made them smarter and their academic work simultaneously less intimidating and more rewarding. Thus began positive feedback loops within themselves, their families, and their school. All kids are curious—just not about the narrow band of ideas that most classrooms offer. Other students are potentially just as capable as Brandon and Vicky of opening themselves up to reading, but we adults haven't made this intellectual pursuit attractive or available enough. Brandon and Vicky realized their curiosity could be satisfied through their passion-reading. Their self-determined, diligent, passion-reading habits fueled their development into the wonderfully complex, thoughtful, high-achieving, gracious kids they are today. When schools take the necessary steps to make intellectual growth more accessible and more attractive to all of our children—not just children primed for a traditional and limited version of academic success—then all of our children will become more successful.

THE STUDENT AND FAMILY PERSPECTIVE

I see every day how access to high-interest books, the time to read, and student choice changes lives. When I have kids tell me how surprised they are at themselves because they used to hate reading, and now they actually ask their moms to take them to the library on the weekend, I know it's changing lives. I know it when I read this in one of my student's Reader's Notebook about their completion of Jerry Spinelli's book *Bully:* "When I read this book I learned that you should not bully kids just because they are not popular and they don't do the stuff you want them to do. When you are not smart or cute like the other kids, you think you're not good enough, but you are. So I know that I won't bully anyone no matter what. Because I don't want other older kids bullying me. I have learned a valuable lesson." I know that student went on a journey that elicited empathy with another person and turned that last page a little more sensitive to the plight of others. When I have kids come back to school on Monday and jump excitedly in my face to tell me about reading two entire books over the weekend, I know they have returned a little bit smarter than when they left on Friday. They have become more curious, more engaged, more empathetic, and more intelligent. What school, teacher, or parent doesn't want that?

THE STUDENT PERSPECTIVE

I sat down individually with the children in my classroom at the end of the school year in June and asked each one to explain his or her reading history to me. I asked them questions such as: *Did you read when you were younger? How do you feel about reading? Have you noticed any changes in your reading habits? Have you noticed any differences in your reading ability? What kinds of books do you like? Do you like choosing books? Have any books given you new goals in life? Do you like read-aloud time?* Here is what the kids had to say:

DAMIR

> I didn't like to read when I was younger; when I was younger I didn't care about reading; I just liked to go outside or play my Xbox or Playstation.
> Reading this year felt good; my head doesn't hurt that much anymore when I read . . . and I read faster. [*What do you mean by your head doesn't hurt that much?*] When I read, sometimes I got frustrated because of a word, but now I understand, because I've learned new words, and I know what they mean and how to pronounce them. I've noticed this year that I've gotten faster and learned big words. I figured out my two favorite genres are poetry and fantasy. I like fantasy because it's just crazy and made up, and poetry because, when I first read poetry when I was little, I began to cry. [*Why would you cry?*] It was just sad.
> Reading has made me want to make more comics, make a new memoir. I want to draw another book. Reading makes me feel kind of happy . . . the characters, how they feel, how the writing is, everything . . . the characters,

how they are emotional, it's like a play in my head. I'm better at reading now, because I'm faster, and I learned new words, pronouncing words, and getting smarter. It just helps my mind think, and I think of different things.

My favorite books are Captain Underpants, Adventure Time, The Regular Show, Lunch Lady, A Poke in the I, The Homework Machine, Animorphs, *and manga books.*

I like that reading helps me get smarter about myself, and it gives me a break from work and having to do everything at once and keep on going, keep on going. I like the read-aloud because it gives me a little break, and I like the poetry, fantasy, memoirs, brain teasers, and it helps me think of new things and gets my mind going . . . and flicks my lightbulb on in my head.

Yes, reading has given me new dreams. I read forty-two books and now I want to become a scientist and a drummer. It helped me think of new cures and helped me become a better person and scientist. Reading Science Fiction, It's Elementary [Putting the Crackle into Chemistry DK], Great Scientists [DK Eyewitness]. *And Albert Einstein is my favorite; he inspired me and he's the one person that made me want to become a scientist. [Why is that?] I like that he thought and cared for people.*

REGGIE

Yes, when I was younger, getting read to a lot had me get a love of reading, and it did help me start to read more. This year I feel great about reading. I feel better, like stronger, than years prior. Well, I'm starting to read more complex books now. My reading has changed. I'm reading more chapter books when I used to read more picture books. I like historical fiction, realistic fiction, biography, autobiography, Jeff Kinney, Dav Pilkey.

I feel like I improved my vocabulary, and it helped my grades improve. I'm starting to understand bigger words. I feel I'm a better reader, because earlier in the year I was reading shorter books, and now I'm reading longer, like three hundred to four hundred page books.

Reading has helped me make up my mind about different places I want to go and different things I want to do when I am older. [Like what?] I want to go to Paris. Books helped me learn more about it. One book I read made me make up my mind that I did want to go to Paris. Goals that reading has given me are for places I want to go and different things that I want to do. Hatchet made me more enthusiastic to go on camping trips, to see how a kid survived with just a hatchet in the woods.

Yes, I love to read. Well, because reading takes me places that I physically wouldn't be able to go. Even if I can't go to a place, or I can't go to Paris or somewhere else, I'd like to go. I can still read a book about someone who has gone there or something about it. When I'm reading it's just me, it makes me happy. Joy. It improves my knowledge, and a lot of books are fun—which is why I love the independent reading we do.

I think being able to choose my own books does help improve my reading by reading what I want to read. Because if teachers just give one thing to read, like these ten books over the year, and that's all you can read, then I think that would not be too fun, that wouldn't make reading fun.

Yes, I like the read-aloud in the morning because it's fun to just, to like, before we start our day, just to sit down and hear you read, and I still like to get read to.

Yes, I will continue to read after this school year, that is something that I will carry on for the rest of my life.

DARIUS

Yes, I liked to read when I was younger. I think this year, reading gave us more freedom, because before when we had SSR we only read for fifteen minutes. Reading was more relaxing this year. I've noticed that the books I read are books that I used to not read in other grades. This year I go for fantasy and historical fiction, when other years I only read realistic fiction. My favorite genre used to be realistic fiction, because the teachers would just give us stuff they got from the computer and stuff, but I stopped liking realistic fiction because it actually kind of got boring, so I went to fantasy, and I liked it, and then I was like, let me try another genre, so I tried histori-cal fiction because the author kind of has predictions in the past about what happened.

My favorite things to read are historical fiction and fantasy, and Rick Riordan, Jeff Kinney, and Raina Telgemeier.

I believe that I'm a better reader now than when I came in the beginning of the year. I think I've improved my reading, because last year I used to not be really as good at decoding, and now that I've read lots of books, now the books have been giving me these more challenging words. I can pick them up now, and I think I'm better at decoding.

Being in fifth grade in our independent reading sessions has changed me over the weekend, because I used to be just in my bedroom just playing video games all day, constant all day, but now that I read books, I read for about two hours a day, I go outside, exercise, relax, then I come back in and have my little relaxing time about six o'clock or so.

Reading actually makes me feel alive, because how some of these authors, they actually have voices in the book, which makes it feel like they are actually talking to you, but they are talking to the other characters. I like these feelings because the books teachers usually assign us to read are usu-ally boring and informational and stuff like that.

Of course I like to read! When we do independent reading, it's kind of like we are just talking in our minds with other characters and predicting the future in the book, it kind of gives you the time to think about what can hap-pen and stuff. My favorite kinds of books are usually things that can teach you something, that is not really real, but can teach you something. Like mythology teaches you about gods, and demigods, and all these things that aren't real, but it gives you a taste of what reading is.

I do like being able to choose my own books. I really think since we can do it, I think other schools should actually do it all around the world. I'm not saying just in the United States, I'm saying every school in the whole entire world to have independent reading time. It basically makes them become smarter in stuff that they really don't know. And I think it's really not fair that some schools just pick stories for other people.

I really like the read-aloud every morning. It kind of warms up our day. It starts the day with something we can listen to and kind of picks up our skills, like paying attention in class, and when read-aloud is happening, sometimes we laugh, so we even get some stuff that we want to talk about during class work time.

I will totally read books over the summer for fun. I might have to limit it to like four hours a day. There are some books that I look at the covers and I think the book is boring, just plain boring, but once I pick it up when I have the free time and I read it, and I notice that the author is using these delicious words, and I figure out that this book is not really boring because of its cover.

I would tell people who don't read, that people that read a lot get smarter and understand things better. I never heard of a scientist that didn't read.

I will totally read after this year, for the rest of my life, and tell my kids, if I have some, that they should read every day and have a great time, but I will always read for the rest of my life. And I think I would actually think of a speech to tell the world that we should actually start reading more instead of goofing around and picking books for kids and stuff, because sometimes when teachers pick books or articles for the kids, they don't get their full education.

EBONY

How I feel about reading this year is that my brain is stronger. I'm learning new words. I feel smarter, because they are bigger books. I noticed I'm developing sounding out words better. And I feel like I improved in taking my time and catching more of the story.

Reading makes me feel that I can be anything, because you have to be a good reader in order to be what you want to be when you grow up. Sometimes the story takes me anywhere . . . that feeling makes me happy, and it feels like I'm in another world.

As you read more books, there are bigger words and more things you can learn, and I like to read because, when you read, you are learning something.

My favorite book is Mockingjay. It was interesting. I like fantasy, realistic fiction, poetry and biography, and also Suzanne Collins and Raina Telgemeier.

Yes, I like being able to choose books, because if you choose what you want, then that means you're actually learning something yourself. If you don't like the book, then you wouldn't have fun reading it.

I like the read-aloud because it reminds me of my mom reading to me. For me, I can picture it more when somebody reads it out loud.

I would say to someone who isn't a reader that you can pick whatever kind of book you want and you can learn from it, and if you read, it will help you get somewhere, because you have to read if you want to get a job. I think reading makes me smarter.

ISIS

Yes, I liked to read when I was younger. I used to read ABC books, but, as I got older, I started reading chapter books, and I really like being read to by an adult, because they put more expression into it.

Reading this year—I feel that it has been a great experience, because at my old school, you had colors for your grade level, and there was a box that you had to choose from, and we weren't as free to read what we wanted. We had to read from that level, but here you can read any book and it's okay, and I like this system.

I've noticed I can read faster this year, because I know more words than I did at the beginning of the year. I can pronounce words better. I feel like this year I improved on reading itself. I can pick up a book and, if there is something I don't know, I read it and start feeling it and start to get the concept or the message.

I discovered I like Sherrilyn Kenyon, because she expresses feeling into her writing that no other writer does. It's like she puts it in as she is experiencing it, so she puts this emotion into it that books really need. She has written Infinity, Invincible, Famous.

Yes, reading has changed my mind about something. Reading historical fiction made me change, like reading Bud, Not Buddy, that made me change my mind about people, because the better you treat them, they might have a better day or a better life. One thing can impact another person's life. You know how he was an orphan? And he went through all that to try to find his father? It surprised me because I don't think anyone would do that, and for him to do that, it made me think he was a good person, so it would be nice to treat other people like that, like he was respectful, and being respectful makes somebody's day and changes what they see.

Reading makes me feel comforted and relaxed, because I get to experience someone's else's world, and I get to take a break from mine. So when I read it feels a whole lot better.

Yes, I do feel like I'm a better reader now than I was at the beginning of the year, because I can grasp everything that I read, like I can take it all in at once and figure it out and put it in different words. At the beginning of the year, I didn't do it. At the beginning of the year, I had to stop after a few paragraphs, so I could get what the author was saying, but now I can take in a whole page or chapter and know what the author is saying automatically.

I love reading a lot, especially when you are having the worst day, you can just pick up a book and the book just makes your day. Say I was in trouble, and I then was really, really mad, and I just picked up a book that relaxes my mind, then I'm just a whole better person. I'm not mad. Like Infinity, I can read that book, and then I feel like, "Oh my gosh, why was I so mad?" I can't even remember. And then that day was just good from that book on.

I like to read because reading gives me a taste of someone else's life, that I will never have, because I am not them. And if I could just live somebody else's life, that would be great, because I can have experiences that I can't have in this life.

My favorite kind of book is a book that makes you want to know what is happening next, like mysteries. They relax your mind so you can focus on just that one thing. I'm like, "Oh my gosh, what is going to happen next?" and I like fantasy, because fantasy is like, "I wish that this would happen in real life," so it's something that you'll never experience.

Sherrilyn Kenyon is my favorite author, because the way she writes her books is like no other. When you read her book, it's like, "Oh my gosh," you'll never get somebody else to write it like that.

I like choosing my own books a lot, because, if it wasn't me choosing freely, then I would not be able to know as much now. I would just know what I'm supposed to know to go to the next grade. But I can learn stuff for now, and also for the next grade. Picking my own books is like letting me choose my feelings, what I want to read. It lets me express my feelings.

[Do you like the read-aloud in the morning?] I love it! Because, like I said earlier, getting read to is awesome. Reading to yourself sometimes can get a little boring, but getting read to you make different voices and stuff, so you make it more fun to read. And I like the read-aloud about world heritage sites. That was interesting, and there are a lot more sites than I thought there were, and reading aloud Sherman Alexie—that was like an experience that no other person had.

After this year ends, yes, I will read for fun. On rainy days or heat waves, or when I don't feel like going anywhere or doing anything, I'll read. I'll even read when I'm on the train.

I would tell someone who isn't a reader that if you read, you'll know more stuff and your knowledge will get better. Say you were really bad at something, then you read and you read and you read, and you'll become better because you'll know more about that.

Something I read that gave me a new goal was Martin Luther King's biography. It made me think about what great things that I am capable of, and how I can set the future to be what it is not now. So I can stop gunfights and stuff like that. And if I didn't read that book, I wouldn't know. He had sisters who were annoying, like mine, and as he gradually got older, he had goals, and he set those goals and he accomplished them, so I can connect that to my life, because I always wanted to go to a great school.

DANIELLE

I like reading books because it's like my mind just loves all the books that I read. When my eyes hurt, my mind is saying "Keep going, I want to know more." I keep on going.

When I was little, I liked to go to the library, and I would pick out any book that I loved to read. My uncle taught me to read, and he would read to me, and then he told me I could read by myself.

Reading makes me feel excited because I get to read books I never heard about before—like Brown Girl Dreaming and El Deafo.

I always read a lot, and whenever I get a chance to read, I try to read every day, every minute, every second, and I will enjoy every minute, every second, and every page I get to read.

My new favorite genres are poetry, traditional, mystery, and sci-fi. I used to only like realistic fiction.

I made a new goal that, instead of reading 40 books, I'm going to try and read 60 books this year, since I already accomplished 50.

Raina Telgemeier books changed my mind. Well, she tells her life story with comic books and that's what I want to do now—be an author now. I want to write books and tell my story of when I was a little girl and how I hated needles back then, and stuff like that. The book Drama *helped me get ready for our play, Shrek Junior, because* Drama *was all about a play her family was doing at the school. So she was like the main character, like I'm the main character in* Shrek Junior, *and it took a lot to remember everything for the play. So when I'm nervous about the play, I just read* Drama *and it helps me feel better. And I like Wes Moore and Jacqueline Woodson.*

Reading makes me feel energetic, excited, and passionate every time I read a new book, and it takes me to a different world, where I really am in that world.

I like that you get a lot of information from books, and it inspires me to do some stuff. Like in Drama *it encouraged me to stand up and ask for some set pieces from other plays. Like I went to see my friend in a play, and I went and talked to the cast director, they said I could borrow some props and scraps from their play to make my play.*

I like to read sci-fi and Scott Westerfield. And poetry just speaks to me and makes me feel good and better.

Yes, I like being able to choose books, because at my old school the teachers made us read some boring books, and it felt like I was always in prison. I never got to choose my own books. Being able to choose your own books is like, "Freedom!" [Danielle dramatically throws her arms wide open], and not being able to is like being in prison. Maybe the teachers just do it so they can make the kids upset, or maybe they think it's a great book, but the kids don't like it. They are probably trying to inspire the kids to read the book. But freedom—you get to read incredible books that you never heard of before: Brown Girl Dreaming, [Discovering] Wes Moore, El Deafo, Guys Read, The Blossoming Universe of Violet Davis, Eggs.

I love the read-aloud every morning because it takes me on a new adventure. While everybody is just sitting at the table, it's like we're sitting on a rollercoaster together listening to the books.

In summer I will probably keep going with my goal and read 70 or 80 books total.

I would tell someone who isn't a reader why they should read is, like, when you read aloud Brown Girl Dreaming, *I was specifically acting like that I was one of Jacqueline Woodson's sisters or little brother, and it really felt like I was in the story. And reading keeps me really calm. I get to breathe; it's like yoga in there. It's like I got a yoga mat, I have a whole yoga station, not literally, but in the other world when I read. I just sit down and "Ommmmm" when I'm reading. And when I'm done reading the book, and that quiet reading time is over, I'm still peacefully calm and excited to read more or go do something else, but I'll still be calm, so I'm not as stressed out as usual.*

Yes! DEFINITELY I will still read for fun. I'm still going after my goal, and if I make it to 100 books when I'm in sixth grade, I will have to stop by here and tell you that I did it. Even if I make it to 80 or 90 that will be good for me.

ISAIAH

When I was younger, I didn't really care as much about reading as I do now. Really, it's because we didn't have interesting books like we do in here.

This year it's GREAT, because I get to read whatever I WANT, and I'm also becoming smarter, like every second, like every minute. I've discovered I like realistic fiction. Usually my favorite kind of books I like are realistic fiction, the ones about middle school, because I want to see what it's going to be like in middle school. One of the books, I think it was Rafe Rules, *helped me avoid fights with a bully. Because in* Rafe Rules, *he was fighting this bully and he got knocked out. So I learned don't mess with bullies, because they're going to mess you up.*

I noticed I can read faster, and I read different books this year. And I'm learning new words. I noticed this year I would have NEVER read those DK Eyewitness *books [nonfiction informational texts] before, I would have never read even one of them before, and I've read A LOT of them this year,* because I wasn't really that interested in books before, so basically books like that got me interested. Reading Percy Jackson made me want to read the [DK Eyewitness] mythology books. I'm definitely a better reader now than at the beginning of the year. I've learned a lot of new words, and like I said before I can read faster.

Reading makes me feel like I'm just in the zone, like sometimes when I read really cool books, I'm just reading, and even if somebody calls me, I'm still reading. It's like when somebody says something in the book, something in quotes, I'm imagining their voice. It's a really great feeling.

I like reading because, in a book, basically whatever you want is just— pick any book, and whatever you want is in there.

My favorite authors are Raina Telgemeier or Christopher Paul Curtis. When we were reading The Watsons Go to Birmingham and Bud, Not Buddy, they were just very detailed, and I could really visualize what they were doing. And Smile and Drama, they were like those high school realistic fiction books.

Picking your own books is basically freedom. You get to read anything that you could ever want, that you could never read before from like first grade to fourth grade, but now I can actually read whatever I want. Kids are the ones that learn from the books they read, and they're also being entertained.

I like the read-aloud, and hearing the poems, the brain teasers, and the books that you read at the end—like Part-Time Indian and Brown Girl Dreaming. It's really good to start the day off with, like with the world heritage sites, because you get to learn about important places all around the world.

Most likely I will read over the summer for fun.

I would tell someone who isn't a reader that they should read because, say you're not that good at reading, it's good practice and you learn to read faster.

[Any new goals?] Well, I've been thinking about being a videogame designer, and making scripts and codes and stuff like that, and I was going *to ask Jarrell for his JavaScript book. I was also thinking about being an inventor, because I read the* Great Scientists *book [DK Eyewitness] and the* Questions and Answers *book. In the future I think I will read some more informational texts.*

JARRELL

I liked to read when I was younger but not as much as I do now. I feel good about reading now, because I can read a lot, and it doesn't take me a long time to finish books. I can read A LOT faster, and I've discovered that I like mysteries and science fiction, and I really like Suzanne Collins. I think I've improved reading more books a year now, and I'm a stronger reader because I read a lot faster.

I notice I read more in my free time. Well, before this year I didn't read in my free time. Every book I read it's like an adventure, because you go to different places and you get to enjoy the places and stuff, and I like to go on those adventures.

My favorite kind of books are the ones that have a good problem and have a place or setting that I have never been to and then the solution where everyone goes their own way. Science fiction and mysteries are the best. I like the Hunger Games Trilogy, NERDS, Revolver.

I like being able to choose books, because I like being given the freedom to read what you like, and when you read what you like, you're going to read more, and that's going to make you a stronger reader and smarter.

I do like the read-aloud, because we get to sit down and enjoy some books and have some mysteries to solve.

I would tell someone who isn't a reader that you should read because you can have a journey to a different place, in a different part of the world, another place you probably have never been to. That's good, because you get to learn about it and solve problems.

I have gotten a goal from reading this computer scripting book, and now I want to become a game designer, like a specialist in scripting.

JADA

I used to not like independent reading, but now I do, because sometimes I think we all need a little break from our work. I also like it because I get to finish up something I read.

I didn't really like to read when I was younger, because there weren't a lot of books that I liked.

I'm reading faster than before, because I was slower, and it would take more time. Reading this year, I feel like I've learned more words. I have improved on reading faster.

I discovered my favorites this year: Sharon Draper and RL Stine, Out of My Mind, The Crystal Camp Code Link, Travel Team, *science-fiction, realistic fiction, biographies, and poetry.*

When I read, I think about things that could've happened but really didn't happen, like real but didn't happen yet. And reading makes me feel happy, because when I'm thinking about something sad, the books help me feel happy again. Something might make me really mad, and then if I just put my anger out on a book, then it helps me, it calms me down. I think I'm a little bit of a better reader now than at the beginning of the year.

I like realistic fiction. I like some sad books, like biographies; sad books can calm you down, and I like reading about people's lives, because if something like that happens to me, I can learn from their life.

Some people don't get to choose because they have to read the same books that the teacher says, but I like to choose, because I like thinking about something else in my mind. You should be able to read anything you want, because it can help you through life. I think having books in the classroom is better, because if you don't have enough to pay for a book, well, at school you get to just take it and bring it back when you're done.

I like the read-aloud because if I see other books I never saw before, then I might want to read it, and this summer if I don't have anything to do, I'll just pick up a book and read.

I would say to someone who doesn't read that if you don't read, then you don't know what will happen if you have a problem. If you read, then you can find out in the book. Like if a person has a problem with their mom, then if the book had the same problem as him, then he could find out what to do.

I will keep reading for fun after this school year, because if I still read, then I can learn more stuff my whole life.

CECE

When I was younger, I would read with my mom at night. I feel reading is fun this year, because at my old school we had to read out of boring textbooks. Both ways are learning, but this way is more fun. It's like I learn more in independent reading, because it's about what I like.

I noticed this year I've started to get more expression when reading. I think I improved my vocabulary too. I noticed usually I read fast, but now I've started to slow down and enjoy what I read.

Since I read The Hunger Games, I've liked science fiction, and seeing what the world could be like. Well, I used to not like science fiction, because I thought it would be a little bit boring, like history, but then I figured out that it's not; it's about the future and all that.

Usually when teachers asked me to read, I would get upset, but now it's fun, especially books I really like. Sometimes when I'm reading, I want to read more. Even during independent reading time, it's enough time, but it's not enough.

Most of the books I used to read were fantasy, but now I like exploring different genres and have decided that I like most of them. My favorite is teenage realistic fiction, because it teaches me what it's like when I grow older. I learned that teenagers get bullied a lot, and most of the time it just says to stay away from them, ignore them, or hang out with other people.

[Any favorite authors or books?] RL Stine, Jacqueline Woodson, Christopher Paul Curtis, Sherman Alexie, Brown Girl Dreaming.

Picking your own books is more useful, because most of the time you learn about history, it's teaching you about history, but it's not relating to things now, and when you read things you like, you learn more words.

I like the books that you pick for read-aloud, because it feels like I know the characters.

I would tell someone who doesn't read that you should, because it's important for your grades, and it's important because you have fun, and you learn more while having fun.

A goal I got from reading this year was that Sherman Alexie makes me want to write a book about real life situations, and things that could happen.

DAJON

I did not like to read when I was younger, but I like reading this year because I like imagining how and why the characters are saying and doing things.

Differences I've noticed this year in reading is that I'm better at understanding the book this year.

I like realistic fiction, like S. A. Bodeen's book The Raft.

I want to go to Paris and France, but then after I read The Raft, I don't want to take a plane [I explained to Dajon at this point how safe airplanes are and that it shouldn't discourage her from flying!]

I like mysteries, and I like getting to the end of the book to see what happens.

Reading makes me feel happy, but it depends on the book. In The Raft I felt sad, because her dad left and her mom was sick, but then I felt happy at the end, because her mom got better and her dad wrote notes to her. It's kind of like you're at the movie theater picturing it in your head, and I like that feeling.

In the beginning of the year, I didn't like reading that much, but now I like realistic fiction.

I like when you read the words and how descriptive it is, so you can imagine it more, and you can think about the people and how they look. When they describe it a lot, it's kind of like customizing, where each part they describe you add it on to the person, and it's like a movie.

I like scary stories, and I like stories that are sad and can make you cry. I like when I stay up and get scared and think about what's going to happen in the book. In sad stories, I like thinking about how I would have felt, and I compare it to how they felt. In one scary story, there was a girl who made a dangerous bet, and I thought that I would never make a bet like that.

My favorite genres are realistic fiction, autobiographies, poetry, and fantasy. I like poetry and rhyming poems, because I want the rhymes to keep going, and I like music, and poetry is helping me when I write my songs.

My favorite books are The Raft, Famous Last Words, *and* Bud, Not Buddy. *And my favorite authors are RL Stine and S. A. Bodeen.*

I do like choosing my own books, because the textbooks aren't that descriptive, and they lose me. The textbooks don't keep me up with the book, because I feel like I get tired reading the textbook.

I like the historic sites book [UNESCO World Heritage Sites] in the read-aloud and when we read Part-Time Indian. *I like how we all get together to read a book; it feels kind of like sometimes you get kind of lonely, because you want to share stuff with people, because you are reading by yourself, but then we all come together, and we can all have a good time reading a book.*

I will read over the summer for fun, and I would tell people that they should read because they can learn new things, and they can find the joy in reading. If you don't read, reading is fun. And if it's raining outside, you have something to occupy yourself.

Reading books did help me think about being a good singer. In one book I read, people kept telling her she shouldn't do this, you should do that, and

> *she should do something else for a living, but when she got older, she met with her friend who played the trumpet for church, and together they made music, and she did wind up singing. Follow your dreams.*

THE FAMILY PERSPECTIVE

Before my students left for the summer, I wanted to gauge if their family members noticed any changes in their child's reading habits over the course of the school year. I knew the changes I had personally witnessed during school, but I wondered how much carried over to my students' home lives. How much of an impact would this daily, intense independent reading and read-aloud have on the children's lives outside of the classroom? Every single family noted improvements in their child's reading enthusiasm during the year, and there were several anecdotes that delighted me. Here are a few:

When I asked Damir's mom if she noticed if he seemed to enjoy reading more this year than other years, she replied "Yes, definitely. He read fifty books! He used to basically do everything he could to not read—like clean his room. Now I see him reading books on mythology on his own . . . and he voluntarily picks up books. I've walked into his room, and now he's really into Minecraft books and graphic novels, and before he wouldn't even look at a book, it was only cartoons or video games . . . just the fact that he picks up a book by himself and will go in his room is a miracle . . . before it was like pulling teeth and bargaining with him: "If you finish the first chapter, you can have a water ice" . . . and he's also spelling better; he also never used to watch anime with my daughter and me, because he would give up on the subtitles, but now he reads along and doesn't give up . . . fluency was a problem before, and now he's reading a lot more fluently, so although he's reading graphic novels and mythology, his reading is a lot better."

And when I asked his mother if she noticed any other changes in Damir's reading habits, she told me: "Just the fact that he reads. I know it sounds mundane, but really, he would not pick up a book . . . even summer reading; just last summer they had *Hatchet*, and it was like pulling teeth just to get him to just go get the book, let alone open it, and now for him to just pick up a book and read it, that's a major change . . . the change is that he reads, asking to go to the library—that's a change. We went to the library before this, but it was so he could go on the computer, and now when we go, he actually will go get a book."

Here is Cece's mom explaining the differences since the school year started: "If it's a book that she enjoys, I can't get it away from her, because she just wants to finish it. And twice I've seen her read a whole book in one day, and I had to make her put it down because she liked it so much—she read it all day, she read it in the car to the restaurant, and I made her stop reading at the restaurant. . . . When she was reading a book, she wanted to know what a word meant, so she took my phone to look up the definition of the word. Normally in school she would read easier books, but now she reads harder books, because they interest her. I asked her where she was going with that big book. And she said, "It was a book I chose." I said, "Did your teacher make you read that book?" She said, "He said I could read whatever book I wanted, and I wanted to read this."

And when I asked Cece's mom if she noticed any other changes with Cece since the beginning of the year, she told me: "Sometimes she will read two or three books at a time. The words she's learned . . . she corrects her sister's sentences, and she corrects mine, and she corrects the sentences we use sometimes and says, 'No, you don't say it this way; you should say it this way,' and she helps me find the words I'm looking for . . . that's new. She's challenging now with her words and her English and her sentences; when she is talking now with the words that she is using, I'm like 'Wow' . . . and my son even says her conversations are becoming more and more intelligent, and I'm like: 'Yes, that's my baby!' So, that lets me know that it's coming from reading."

Speaking of the reading we do in school, Reggie's mom told me: "It's more important, because a lot of kids don't read over the summer, and a lot of kids don't read over the weekend . . . and I think because they read so much here, but giving them books that they like, so it's more interesting, and not what the school wants them to do." And when I asked her if she ever sees Reggie voluntarily reading on the weekend, she said, "He has some books from Scholastic, so a lot of times some of those books, and a book from school." She added that his reading habits are "getting greater, because he's more excited about reading more; he's more excited about the titles."

When I asked Danielle's grandmother if there were any changes she had noticed, she told me: "Yes, just last week I asked her to read, and I have seen a great deal of improvement in the way she reads . . . [I've been] very pleased with the progress and the books that she's got. And it's a big difference, because Danielle did not like to read in the beginning, then this year she is constantly. If she is not reading a book, she is on the internet reading. She has really changed on her reading, and I am very, very pleased with that . . . In the kitchen she took out a book she likes reading, and she was explaining to me what type of book it was and everything, and she had never broken it down to me before and told me about her reading material. And it's nice to see that Danielle, she has really improved this year about her reading and I really enjoy hearing her read to me. She is a lot stronger than last year."

Isaiah's mom noticed this change: "How animated he is, how expressive he is when he is reading . . . [his reading is] even more improved this year than it was before. He loves it more, especially when people say he's doing so well; he loves that." She also noticed a change on the weekend: "He just picks up books on the weekend."

When I asked Jada's mom if she had seen any changes she replied, "Yes, definitely. I always see her reading. When she has never been asked to read, she reads. And, also, she comprehends more, and she actually talks about it. She tells me about the story; when she engages me into the story or tells me that she wants to read to me—that's different." And Jada's mom said another change she had noticed was Jada reading about "teenagers and going through teenager things, and she's really engulfed in that book on her own time. And she travels with a book sometimes; if we go places, she brings a book with her. I noticed that she has an excessive amount of books in her book bag . . . She will read one book and then later read a different one . . . She is reading multiple books at one time."

When I asked Darius's dad if he had noticed any changes in his son's reading habits this year, he put it like this: "Yes, whenever we go somewhere he brings a book with him, and when we ride somewhere he has his book; visiting family he takes a book with him; he always has a book with him; when he's not doing too much of anything, having a little snack, he reads. I noticed that he puts his game down a little more and he reads. I do notice that he does read more, that he's active, like he's in this mode to read. He talks about what he's read, and he's actually gathering information from what he's reading. I think he comprehends a lot more of what he's reading. He can actually give you specifics, and I think he gets more depth out of reading now. It's exciting enough to me to see him take a book; when we're ready to go somewhere he wants to bring a book. I like that. And then after he reads so much in a day, he'll sit down and give me information about what he read. It's not one specific subject; it's random titles, all kinds of different things—biographies, information regarding cities or states, and then he goes to fiction. He reads a lot. That was kind of a surprise for me—to see him walk down the steps and ball up with a book and read."

Dajon's mom explained to me, when I asked her if she noticed whether Dajon seemed to enjoy reading more this year, "Yes, a lot more. When she was in fourth grade, her teacher expressed how important reading was, and I said to her that Dajon really didn't like to read, and it was hard for me to get her to read a book—compared to this year, where she is coming home telling me about the different sci-fi books she's reading, and I see them in her book bag, and she's reading them in the car." She also added that she thinks Dajon reads "a lot better, and I see the change in the books that she's reading. She reads in the car, and if I'm listening to a station she doesn't particularly care to listen to, she'll get her book out of the car and start reading. Or watching TV, if it's something she doesn't care to watch, she'll pick up a book and read. She does it on her own. It's the reading more; even if it's not a book, it's reading articles she's interested in. She's very interested in art, so she'll look it up on her phone, and I see she's reading an article on how to do different designs and how this started out. She is actually taking an interest in reading up on them and how to do this on her own."

READING PROFICIENCY AND VOCABULARY DEVELOPMENT

From the students' and families' perspectives, the children clearly read more often, improved their reading ability, and enjoyed reading more. In addition to interviewing the students and parents, we thought it would be informative to collect data on the student's reading proficiency and vocabulary development. To measure the efficacy of a school year with a daily 120 minutes of independent reading and 30 minutes of teacher read-aloud time, we collected data from the 2nd Edition of the *Developmental Reading Assessment* (DRA2), and measured vocabulary development using the 4th Edition of the *Expressive One-Word Vocabulary Test*.

As explained in the manual, "The DRA2, 4-8, assesses student performance in the following areas of reading proficiency: Reading

Engagement, Oral Reading Fluency, and Comprehension. The selection of these target skill areas and the methods used to assess them are based on current research in reading from sources such as the National Reading Panel Report (2000) and Reading for Understanding (Rand Education, 2002)." We used the DRA2 data from May 2014 (end of 4th grade school year), September 2014 (beginning of 5th grade school year), and June 2015 (end of 5th grade school year). The only data missing was from 2 new students in 5th grade who did not take the DRA2 in 4th grade at their previous school.

As the manual also explains, "The Expressive One-Word Vocabulary Test, 4th Edition (EOWPVT-4), is an individually administered, norm-referenced assessment of an individual's ability to name objects, actions, and concepts when presented with color illustrations. It was standardized on English-speaking individuals ages 2 through 80+ years residing in the United States." This assessment was individually given to each student in October 2014 (beginning of 5th grade school year) and in June 2015 (end of 5th grade school year).

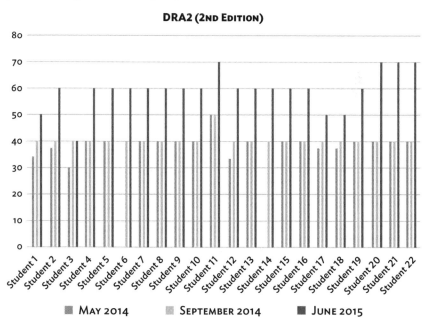

DRA2 (2ND EDITION)

Pre and Post Test—DRA2 and Expressive One-Word Vocabulary

	DRA2 (2nd Edition)			Expressive One-Word Vocabulary (4th Edition)			
				Age Equivalent		Percentile Rank	
	May 2014	Sept. 2014	June 2015	Oct. 2014	June 2015	Oct. 2014	June 2015
Student 1	34	40	50	10-8	11-8	50	53
Student 2	38	40	60	10-8	12-0	53	63
Student 3	30	40	40	10-10	12-8	37	53
Student 4	40	40	60	11-2	12-6	58	73
Student 5	40	40	60	11-8	13-3	68	81
Student 6	NA	40	40	8-6	11-4	19	53
Student 7	40	40	60	11-10	14-0	70	88
Student 8	40	40	60	13-3	14-6	87	91
Student 9	40	40	60	11-10	12-10	70	73
Student 10	40	40	60	11-4	12-0	73	70
Student 11	50	50	70	12-8	16-9	77	96
Student 12	34	40	60	10-2	12-8	39	66
Student 13	40	40	60	11-0	13-0	53	70
Student 14	NA	40	60	9-2	11-8	32	58
Student 15	40	40	60	12-3	12-0	79	68
Student 16	40	40	60	14-0	17-11	90	98
Student 17	38	40	50	11-6	11-8	63	53
Student 18	38	40	50	7-6	7-10	10	9
Student 19	40	40	60	11-2	11-10	61	61
Student 20	40	40	70	10-10	12-10	53	73
Student 21	40	40	70	11-2	11-6	58	50
Student 22	40	40	70	11-2	12-8	50	61

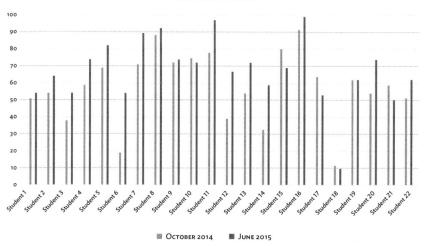

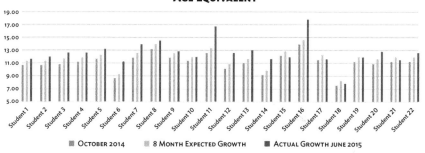

RESULTS FOR THE DRA AND EXPRESSIVE ONE-WORD VOCABULARY

1. DRA

The means and standard deviations for the DRA in May 2014, September 2014, and June 2015 are presented in table 1. Since there is some missing data, two sets of scores are presented: for all subjects and then for those subjects who have complete data for all three data points.

Table 1: DRA Means and (Standard Deviations)

MAY, 2014		SEPTEMBER, 2014		JUNE, 2015	
All Subjects	Subjects with Complete Data	All Subjects	Subjects with Complete Data	All Subjects	Subjects with Complete Data
39.10 (3.75)	39.10 (3.75)	40.45 (2.13)	40.50 (2.24)	58.64 (8.35)	59.50 (7.59)

A one-way, repeated measures ANOVA was computed on the above data. This produced a highly significant result ($F = 173.58$, $p = .000$, partial eta squared = .901). All of the comparisons among the means were significant. Since the focus is more than likely on the September to June data, the data were run again on only this comparison. As before, the result was highly significant ($F = 115.068$, $p = .000$, partial eta squared = .846).

2.   Expressive One-Word Vocabulary Test—Age Equivalent Data

The means and standard deviations for the age equivalent scores are presented in table 2. The age equivalent data were converted to months for analysis.

Table 2: Age Equivalent Scores

OCTOBER, 2014	JUNE, 2015
133.18 (17.19) (Approximately 11-1)	152.23 (23.63) (Approximately 12-7)

The repeated measures ANOVA produced a highly significant result ($F = 43.721$, $p = .000$, partial eta squared = .676).

3.   Expressive One-Word Vocabulary Test—Percentile Rank Data

The means and standard deviations for the percentile rank scores are presented in table 3.

Table 3: Percentile Rank Scores

OCTOBER, 2014	JUNE, 2015
56.82 (20.46)	66.41 (19.20)

The repeated measures ANOVA produced a significant result ($F = 13.38$, $p = .001$, partial eta squared = .389).

It shouldn't be surprising, when you personally read over 40 books in 9 months, and someone reads high-level poetry and prose aloud to you for 180 school days, that your reading proficiency and vocabulary improve in statistically significant ways—but it's still nice to have the data confirm it.

• • •

Recurring Themes in Student Achievement

RECURRING THEMES IN STUDENT ACHIEVEMENT	HOW NARRATIVE IMMERSION ADDRESSES
1. Emotional well-being in the classroom is paramount.	By building a genuine empathetic community during daily read-aloud time
2. Students need positive, nurturing relationships with their teachers.	Through read-aloud time, individual conferencing, audiobook check-ins
3. Students need clear and consistent feedback.	Through conferencing, book talks, audiobook check-ins
4. Students need to develop cultural literacy, building background knowledge in order to contextualize new information more easily.	Through wide exposure to cultural literacy during read-aloud and the steady build-up of background knowledge during independent reading and listening to audiobooks
5. Students respond well to high expectations for reaching achievable goals.	By establishing at the beginning of the year the firm goal of reading a minimum of 40 books by the end of the year
6. Intrinsic motivation produces better results than extrinsic motivation.	By allowing class personality and class interest to help guide read-aloud and audiobook selections and by letting students choose their own books for independent reading
7. Student learning is enhanced by the development of individual agency, a growth mindset, and an internal locus of control.	By consistently reminding students that every minute they spend reading makes them incrementally smarter and that the way to excel academically is to read for thousands of hours
8. Thousands of hours of deliberate, authentic practice are necessary for mastery.	By combining 120 minutes of independent reading and/or audiobook support and 30 minutes of read-aloud per day

CHAPTER 7

NURTURING BOOK LIFE IN A DIGITAL WORLD

We are drowning in information, while starving for wisdom.

~ E.O. WILSON

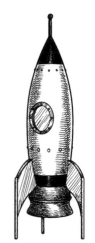

DIGITAL LIFE VERSUS BOOK LIFE

t's impossible to discuss reading without discussing its direct competitor—digital life. Our kids' lives are dominated by video games and social media, and there are facets to both that need to be explored. I personally grew up playing video games with my friends in arcades, basements, and bedrooms. Hanging out, laughing, joking, and trash-talking with friends while playing video games is a great time. There is nothing inherently wrong with the games, but the issue is that kids are more physically isolated from their friends when they play and thus playing more games alone. There are positive aspects of the social video-game experience that make it worthwhile, but if books are generally more about switching on, then the solitary video-games experience is generally more about switching off. Switching off and escaping every once in a while is perfectly healthy, but too many of our kids play video games by themselves excessively and it's not helping them progress academically, socially, or emotionally.

Anthropologist Natasha Schüll has described people mesmerized by slot machines as being in "the machine zone." And writer Alexis Madrigal says this is the dark side of flow. He writes, "The games exploit the human desire for flow, but without the meaning or mastery attached to the state. The machine zone is where the mind goes as the body loses itself in the task." Madrigal goes on to connect the machine zone to the popularity of social media. And this brings us back to the educational goal of mastery. Flow is a very desirable mental state; it allows us to focus intensely on the task at hand. But there is a discrepancy between the flow state of narrative immersion and the "dark flow" state of video games and social media. Reading has a much higher learning curve, but once you pass a certain inflection point, you can slip more easily into that narrative-immersion flow state. But since the reading learning curve is so much higher than that of video games, many children become frustrated with it, experience it negatively, and associate it with tedium and drudgery—to such a degree that they give up before they actually master the reading process. If you expand the spectrum of books in your classroom and give students the choice to read what resonates personally, they will be intrinsically motivated to challenge themselves. Reading simply demands more of you cognitively in ways that digital media do not. If we help children conquer the high learning curve of reading, the world of the reading flow-state—and with it positive academic growth—can be theirs.

Joan Didion writes, "We tell ourselves stories in order to live." Life without stories is not an option. Our brains are wired for narrative, and we not only crave stories—but also we need them to make sense of the world. Everything is narrative. And if we don't provide our children with compelling narratives at home and at school, narratives from questionable sources will surely fill that void. Video games, television, and social media all provide stories as well, just not the kind of stories we want our kids to use as building blocks as they construct their values and understanding of the world.

The problem is that when we consume stories created solely as a source of revenue, without regard for artistic quality, we are not going to receive the most nuanced, complex, or elevated content. We will frequently receive content that catalogs failure and degradation. Of course, there can be great shows and bad books, but the written long-form narrative is more likely than digital media to offer more empathic journeys of understanding other people. And we can curate our classroom libraries to make sure that our kids have exposure to the great books. All stories are not created equal. Kids will play games, scroll web pages, and watch shows, but we need to provide the counterbalance in school. Too many children consume only exploitative media content designed solely to attract attention, so that content is what they prefer. If we give literature an equal shot—as we must— literature will win.

The lure of this machine zone is magnetic. Having grown up with video games, I am intimately aware of their power. And I can allow myself to become just as mesmerized by the dark flow of video games and social media as the kids do. A long time ago, I began to notice particular feelings after playing video games that were quite different from how I felt after reading an engaging story. Emerging from a longer video-game session always left me with a sense of gnawing hollowness, whereas emerging from a longer reading session always left me in a satisfied, reflective state. Both experiences require one to take a few moments afterward to readjust to the real world, but the reading flow-state is decidedly better.

The fundamental difference between the reading zone and the machine zone is that the reading zone is a world you personally create, while the machine zone is one to which you passively submit. The story that you read depends entirely upon you to construct it, whereas most video games are constructed without your involvement. You feel different after you read, because you have participated actively in the creative construction of the story. A typical video game invites you to be a passive receptacle for effortless pleasure. Accepting that invitation can be relaxing, but it never moves you forward. I tend to feel marginal growth after reading, while feeling only empty static after playing video games. The game may have been extremely engaging while it lasted, but I'm in the same place afterward as I when I started. Video games give you novelty and capture your attention, but it is more of an inert flow than a growth flow.

Several years ago, I started to notice that many of my students got their background knowledge from video games. The popular game series *Assassin's Creed* particularly stood out to me. The kids would be familiar with certain historical figures and also the cities of Florence, Rome, and Paris because they were used as settings in the game. I was initially excited that they had this background knowledge but soon realized there was a very real imaginative gap between background knowledge gained digitally and that gained through literature.

If you play a detailed video game that is set in Paris, you can have an interesting adventure that can give you a general familiarity with the city. Reading something well-written about Paris, on the other hand, engages your imagination in a way that requires you to fully participate. It requires you to construct in your mind the setting's entire range of sounds, sights, and scents. The digital Paris has been constructed without your participation.

Going to Paris in a video game is similar to visiting the Las Vegas version of the city—it might be somewhat interesting, but it would pale in comparison to reading a well-written descriptive portrait of Paris and creating that Paris in your mind. There is a qualitative difference between the video-game/Las Vegas simulacrum of Paris and the city encountered in a richly detailed story about Paris. Because the story you read of Paris relies on you for its construction, it's going to be shaped in a very personal way in your imagination. That well-written story will be more evocative than the real-life imitation because you created it. Literature is more intimate than the real-life imitation. And that intimacy is more compelling than the simulacrum. When you read fluently enough and become an active participant in its construction, the world of a story depends entirely upon you to create it and give it meaning. The Paris of your imagination is richer than the Paris of Las Vegas.

It's for this reason that reading increases your wonder and fascination with the world in ways that I have not experienced or witnessed with video games. For this reason also, the intimacy of reading is more conducive to real life change and progress. Reading about Paris is more likely to inspire you to visit Paris than playing a video game. So when family members tell me that they have seen their children voluntarily spending time reading that previously would have been spent playing video games I know something real has been accomplished.

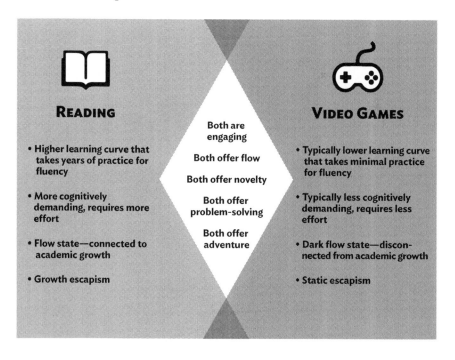

READING

- Higher learning curve that takes years of practice for fluency

- More cognitively demanding, requires more effort

- Flow state—connected to academic growth

- Growth escapism

Both are engaging

Both offer flow

Both offer novelty

Both offer problem-solving

Both offer adventure

VIDEO GAMES

- Typically lower learning curve that takes minimal practice for fluency

- Typically less cognitively demanding, requires less effort

- Dark flow state—disconnected from academic growth

- Static escapism

SOCIAL MEDIA VS. SOCIAL LITERACY

Perpetual stimulation without satisfaction, becomes imprisoning.
~ JONATHAN FRANZEN

We all have seen children and adults grow demented in the glow of their black mirrors. Social media can be very bleak. Social literacy activities like read-aloud, book talks, Kindles with audio, can counter that despair. Read-aloud is ultimately an exploratory cooperative dialectic. The teacher's reading selections provide a framework, but what transpires is original, fresh, and improvised, based on the individual members of your class. The virtue of this is that you have this beautifully built-in Socratic dialogue happening every morning. Ideas from a diverse array of human experiences are presented through poetry and prose. The class susses out questions in real time, and, as individuals, we each make meaning. Unlike the edited life of social media, the unedited life of read-aloud leads to discovery. The unedited misunderstandings lead us to clarification and make up a communal journey. It's the unscripted that provides our opportunity of discovery—discovery of knowledge and discovery of each other.

It's difficult to properly convey how moving and powerful—how meaningful—a read-aloud session can be in a classroom. For example, I just had several kids ask me to read *The Fault in Our Stars* by John Green. A few had seen the movie and asked if I would read the book aloud to them. I bought a copy of the book, and as I read the book to them (careful to not read the rare inappropriate word or passage) the class became enamored. I could tell this was a special moment for our class. *The Fault in Our Stars* is a beautifully told story about a teenage girl living with her cancer diagnosis. There is much more than that going on in the book, but what happened in my classroom was even more interesting. Boys and girls were equally gripped by the story and our shared journey through the book together. We discussed the characters, the settings, the plot, and metaphors; we reread important passages to clarify exactly what happened; we defined words like *precariously, ubiquitous,* and *idyllic;* we laughed out loud; and we were silently moved. When you look around the room and see every single one of your students engaged in this collective journey as you read the book aloud, when the kids beg you to read one more chapter, you know something larger than the academics—something more elevated—is transpiring. I know everyone in the classroom was projecting the feelings of loved ones lost, loved ones battling cancer or disease, and imagining how their loved one might be feeling and how they felt about their loved one. The book is ultimately about meaning-making, and the book answers far-reaching questions the children wanted answered. The book is about mortality and why we are here, and how you make the best life possible with the limited time you have. How do you make this life meaningful as you stumble through it? As we passed our time in the dark, *The Fault in Our Stars* became a candle for our class. We were collectively in the zone, and reading that book together became existentially significant in ways that will never be felt with grammar-rule practice or comprehension worksheets.

You could click a few times and participate in online discussions about *The Fault in Our Stars,* but that is an empty experience compared to the fullness of sitting in the same room with people you care about, sharing the experience together as a class. There is nothing quite like the power of social literacy. Books espouse values. And when you gather together around a table and share great stories, it is an undeniably powerful experience.

Sherry Turkle is a sociologist, psychologist, technology expert, and professor at MIT. She has written extensively about what's at stake when we shift increasing portions of our lives to digital screens and away from human faces. Here are some astute thoughts from her book *Reclaiming Conversation:*

Face-to-face conversation is the most human—and humanizing—thing
we do. Fully present to one another, we learn to listen. It's where we develop
the capacity for empathy. It's where we experience the joy of being heard, of
being understood. And conversation advances self-reflection, the conver-
sations with ourselves that are the cornerstone of early development and
continue throughout life.

It all adds up to a flight from conversation—at least from conversation
that is open-ended and spontaneous, conversation in which we play with
ideas, in which we allow ourselves to be fully present and vulnerable. Yet
these are the conversations where empathy and intimacy flourish and social
action gains strength.

Time in simulation gets children ready for more time in simulation.
Time with people teaches children how to be in a relationship, beginning
with the ability to have a conversation. And this brings me back to the anxi-
eties of the Holbrooke teachers. As the Holbrooke middle schoolers began to
spend more time texting, they lost practice in face-to-face talk. That means
lost practice in the empathic arts—learning to make eye contact, to listen,
and to attend to others. Conversation is on the path towards the experience
of intimacy, community, and communion. Reclaiming conversation is a
step towards reclaiming our most fundamental human values.

A daily read-aloud in every classroom is the place to start reclaiming conversation. When we come together in our classroom as a school
family, our family dinner is the read-aloud. Each morning I greet all the
kids as they walk in the room and gather around the big table by the
windows. If it's bright enough outside, we keep the fluorescent lights off
and just use the natural light and a few lamps to illuminate the room
warmly. Everyone sits around at eye-level, facing each other, radiating
out from the pile of books in in the middle.

To demonstrate how much can happen in just 30 minutes of read-
aloud every morning, I will walk through our last two mornings. I always

start with a few poems. One of the poems I read yesterday was this one by Jacqueline Woodson from *Brown Girl Dreaming*.

My Mother Looks Back on Greenville

After our dinner and bath,
after our powdered and pajamaed bodies are tucked
three across into bed,
after Winnie the Pooh and kisses on our foreheads
and longer-than-usual hugs,

my mother walks away from the house on Hall Street
out into the growing night,
down a long dusty road
to where the Nicholtown bus
takes her to the Greyhound station

then more dust
then she's gone.

New York ahead of her,
her family behind, she moves
to the back, her purse in her lap,
the land
pulling her gaze into the window once more.
Before darkness
covers it and for many hours, there are only shadows

and stars
and tears
and hope.

We didn't dissect that poem line by line. We just enjoyed the rhythm, the imagery, and the sentiment. We read a brain teaser from the book *One-Minute Mysteries and Brain Teasers*, made our guesses, and then read the solution. We read from Lonely Planet's *The Travel Book: A Journey Through Every Country in the World*, where we looked at photos and read brief descriptions and interesting facts about each country. Yesterday, it was about South Korea and kimchi, how South Korea differs from North Korea, falafel and hummus in Kuwait, yurts and horse sausages in Kyrgyzstan, and slurping pho in Laos, with lots of comments about how delicious a warm noodle soup like pho would be on a cold rainy day like the one outside our windows.

Next, we looked at photos from *A Complete Guide to UNESCO World Heritage Sites*. We saw a photo of Gaudi's *La Sagrada Familia* in Barcelona, Spain; the Konark Sun Temple in India; Yosemite National Park; the Statue of Liberty; Iguazu National Park in Argentina; Lake Malawi National Park in Malawi; the remains of the Temple of Jupiter in Lebanon; and The Canadian Rocky Mountain Park in Canada. They all looked at the photos as I read the captions.

One of my students, Brigette, brought in the book *Don't Sweat the Small Stuff* and *It's All Small Stuff: Simple Ways to Keep the Little Things from Taking Over Your Life*, by Richard Carlson. She really liked the book and requested I read it aloud. We read the second selection, which is about always striving to do your very best to improve, and yet also make peace with imperfection. The author says that when we are overly focused on our imperfections or others' imperfections, it takes us away from being kind and gentle. We want to realize ways to improve life, and always strive to do our best, but not be consumed with what's wrong. I explained to the class how it reminds me of what Martin Luther King Jr., said when he spoke about having "a tough mind and a tender heart" and about how combining these seemingly contrary virtues provides us with the proper balance. Danielle then brought up her yin-yang symbol necklace which represents opposites in harmony and how that's similar too.

When I read the introduction to *Don't Sweat the Small Stuff*, I included the William James quotation: "The greatest discovery of my generation is that a human being can alter his life by altering his attitude." When the kids asked who he was, I said that he studied philosophy, psychology, and physiology and tried to blend them together in his thinking. They wanted to know what philosophy was, so I told them it's kind of like the study of the meaning of life, like how we should live and how we should act. They asked me if I had any philosophy books, so I pulled off the shelf a book literally called *The Philosophy Book: Big Ideas Simply Explained*. I read a quote by Plato, which led at first to some jokes about his name being *Play-Doh* and then to an explanation of Plato's allegory of the cave, which I connected to what we read the previous day about the living conditions in North Korea and how you could say the people see only the shadows in the cave, because they have no knowledge of the outside world. Then there was another quotation in *The Philosophy Book* from Shakespeare: "There is nothing either good or bad, but thinking makes it so," and then we recognized how similar it was to the one by William James about altering your life by altering your attitude.

Then we settled in to read from *The Fault in Our Stars*. Some of my students really love to sit on the carpet with a pillow to listen to me read the prose aloud, so I let them slip out of their chairs and spill onto the floor. Some of the things that came up in the chapter we read were Amsterdam, the Rijksmuseum, canals, houseboats, Anne Frank, Anne's father Otto Frank, how you could possibly go on living after losing your whole family as he did, the Holocaust, Nazis, the Gestapo, genocide, and concentration camps. I could tell that my kids were hearing about virtually all of these things for the first time. And as soon as I finished the read-aloud, the kids automatically went to grab the World War II

DK Eyewitness book off the shelf to learn more about Anne Frank and World War II.

This morning I began with more poems, including this one by Jacqueline Woodson called "The Last Fireflies."

> *We know our days are counted here.*
> *Each evening we wait for the first light*
> *of the last fireflies, catch them in jars*
> *then let them go again. As though we understand*
> *their need for freedom.*
> *As though our silent prayers to stay in Greenville*
> *will be answered if*
> *we do what we know is right.*

After the poems, we read a *One-Minute Mystery*, and in *The Travel Book*, we learned that pig's snout is a traditional Christmas dish in Latvia, that baklava is a popular treat in Lebanon, and that Lesotho is completely landlocked by South Africa. In the *World Heritage Sites* book we saw a picture of ancient columns and ruins in Lebanon; a Mosque-Cathedral in Córdoba, Spain; Burgos Cathedral in Spain; the Alhambra in Granada, Spain; monuments in Mahabalipuram, India; the Historic District of Quebec, Canada; bright, multicolored homes in Brazil, and the Roman Aqueduct of Segovia, Spain. We read an explanation of what an aqueduct is, and then we collectively marveled at the durability of something built 2,000 years ago.

We read the third selection in *Don't Sweat the Small Stuff*, which was about how fearful, frantic thinking drains us, and how, counterintuitively, becoming more gentle and relaxed actually helps us achieve more in life. *The Philosophy Book* mentioned how thousands of years ago in Greece some theorized that, because water is essential to life, capable of motion, and capable of change, water must be the basic material of the cosmos.

The chapter we read from *The Fault in Our Stars* discussed Maslow's Hierarchy of Needs, hamartia, how you face surprising tragic news, how you face sickness and death, how you live the best life possible, what gallows humor is, and what an honorable death is.

This incredibly broad range of knowledge covered in just two typical read-aloud sessions is powerful for a reason. I could have given my students worksheets with the terms I mentioned above or maybe expository paragraphs explaining everything above, but the knowledge would never stick the way it sticks when it is embedded in an authentic story. There was nothing contrived about what we did together as a class. We sat together to read a variety of genres, stretching the kids above their reading level, exploring and connecting ideas, and settling into a great story that interested them. That is a social, autotelic experience. The learning flowed from an authentic, pleasurable, and academically potent source. That is why they don't want our read-aloud time to end. That is why the school day and school year fly by. And they will remember more about Anne Frank from *The Fault in Our Stars* than from any worksheet I could ever give them.

None of these connections were planned. I selected great books for read-aloud, kids expressed interest in certain directions, and I did my best to take them there. The connections naturally happen when you combine great books, the kids' interests, and a teacher willing to lead the expedition. When we read about the countries of the world, kids naturally chime in with their family relations from other countries, and fill us in on family stories, proper pronunciations, and traditions they may be familiar with. In this year's class, the kids had family members who either immigrated from or currently reside in India, Finland, Ghana, Kenya, France, Sierra Leone, the Netherlands, Cambodia, the United Kingdom, Jamaica, Ireland, Italy, Indonesia, and Puerto Rico. We share and learn things about each other we would otherwise never know. And that builds trust—which, in turn, builds love and respect.

The read-aloud is a live, improvisational performance. You have your appropriate books preselected, and then the group interacts with the reading. Sometimes it falls a little flat, but most days the group discussion is insightful, poignant, humorous, and tender. You lay a foundation of interesting background knowledge and compelling stories, and the connections are made in a natural way. Exposing the students to so much, touching on so many topics, locations, and ideas—something always captures every child's interest. You pique their curiosity, and expose them to the broad range of what the world offers. There is ample opportunity for the kids to share during the read-aloud, just as there is in an authentic conversation. You share your books as a teacher, students share their books during book talks, and everyone shares their thoughts. The teacher guides the conversation and makes sure everyone is respectful and engaged.

Reading about the cathedrals in the *World Heritage Sites* book reminds me of that anecdote about a man walking down the street and seeing two stonemasons doing exactly the same job. The man asks the masons what they are doing. The first mason says, "I'm breaking stones." The second mason replies, "I'm building a cathedral."

We can perceive the same undertaking in perfectly diametric ways. This applies to teaching as well. If you were to observe those read-aloud sessions from a breaking stones perspective, you could say that I was modeling, instructing, and formatively assessing the following Common Core State Standards:

CCSS.ELA-LITERACY.RL.5.2

Determine a theme of a story, drama, or poem from details in the text, including how characters in a story or drama respond to challenges or how the speaker in a poem reflects upon a topic; summarize the text.

CCSS.ELA-LITERACY.RL.5.4

Determine the meaning of words and phrases as they are used in a text, including figurative language such as metaphors and similes.

CCSS.ELA-LITERACY.RL.5.9
Compare and contrast stories in the same genre (e.g., mysteries and adventure stories) on their approaches to similar themes and topics.

CCSS.ELA-LITERACY.RF.5.3.A
Use combined knowledge of all letter-sound correspondences, syllabication patterns, and morphology (e.g., roots and affixes) to read accurately unfamiliar multisyllabic words in context and out of context.

CCSS.ELA-LITERACY.RF.5.4.B
Read grade-level prose and poetry orally with accuracy, appropriate rate, and expression on successive readings.

CCSS.ELA-LITERACY.SL.5.1
Engage effectively in a range of collaborative discussions (one-on-one, in groups, and teacher-led) with diverse partners on *grade 5 topics and texts*, building on others' ideas and expressing their own clearly.

CCSS.ELA-LITERACY.SL.5.1.B
Follow agreed-upon rules for discussions and carry out assigned roles.

CCSS.ELA-LITERACY.SL.5.1.C
Pose and respond to specific questions by making comments that contribute to the discussion and elaborate on the remarks of others.

CCSS.ELA-LITERACY.SL.5.2
Summarize a written text read-aloud or information presented in diverse media and formats, including visually, quantitatively, and orally.

If you were to observe those read-aloud sessions from the building cathedrals perspective, you would say the children were engaged, comfortable, and happy. You would say they were building empathy, relationships, trust, wonder, and wisdom. You would say they were learning in an optimally engaged flow state. The problem with interjecting tedious jargon is that it disrupts the autotelic process. The unnecessary corrupts the learning. There is nothing to be gained by gumming up the flow with technical rhetoric or extraneous comprehension worksheets. When technical rhetoric and comprehension worksheets occupy too much of the school experience, our children associate learning with technical rhetoric, comprehension worksheets, and drudgery. Kids need to be inspirationally focused on building cathedrals every day, not breaking stones. And the social literacy experience of read-aloud is the cornerstone of inspiration.

When you decide to share something about your life with someone, you are saying you trust that person enough to reveal whatever it is you reveal. That builds friendship and intimacy. When you post something on social media, however, in a sense you are freely giving it away, and you lose it. When you indiscriminately post your business on social media, you devalue it. There is nothing inherently wrong with posting something, but when you have more intimate real-world relationships with people with whom you selectively disclose information, you create trust and empathy. Social media blasts may garner attention but not necessarily trust and empathy. Social media is more about presentation than authenticity, and managing your public persona is not the same thing as managing your identity. It is difficult to put into words how meaningful read-aloud can be. The combination of expertly written stories about real-life matters, shared around a table full of engaged people, sharing their opinions in a thoughtful, kind way, creates a certain kind of magic. An authentic magic that is built into every single school day.

SOLID VS. HOLLOW

As Aristotle said, the poet is greater than the historian because he presents not only things as they were, but foreshadows what they might have been. We forsake literature when we are content to chronicle disaster. Tragedy, therefore, is inseparable from a certain modest hope regarding the human animal. And it is the glimpse of this brighter possibility that raises sadness out of the pathetic toward the tragic.

~ ARTHUR MILLER

A lot of what constitutes our media, be it social media or traditional media, is simply content to chronicle disaster. When we read poetry and prose every morning in the classroom and share with each other what is meaningful to us through book talks, we give children the opportunity to delve into the books that they personally choose to answer their questions. When we do that, we move to contextualize tragedy instead of merely chronicling disaster. When we give our children the time every day to read independently, we give them a uniquely personalized education. And when we give them read-aloud sessions and book-talks every day, we are giving them a connective social education. By combining both the introspective autotelic learning and the extrospective autotelic learning, we are helping students internalize lifelong learning habits. Tedious, grinding worksheets and meaningless digital novelties are hollow. Flow is solid. These are fundamentally different pursuits. We need to help our students to experience social and introspective flow in their learning every single day.

Here Csikszentmihalyi elaborates on Emile Durkheim's concepts of anomie and alienation, which are very relevant to understanding student discomfort and disengagement in school. They are also very relevant to understanding the discomfort and disengagement students feel when their schools and lives become too digital:

> Two terms describing states of social pathology apply also to conditions
> that make flow difficult to experience: anomie and alienation. Anomie—lit-
> erally, "lack of rules"—is the name the French sociologist Emile Durkheim
> gave to a condition in society in which the norms of behavior had become
> muddled. When it is no longer clear what is permitted and what is not,
> when it is uncertain what public opinion values, behavior becomes erratic
> and meaningless. People who depend on the rules of society to give order to
> their consciousness become anxious. Anomic situations might arise when
> the economy collapses, or when one culture is destroyed by another, but
> they can also come about when prosperity increases rapidly, and old values
> of thrift and hard work are no longer as relevant as they had been.
>
> Alienation is in many ways the opposite: it is a condition in which people
> are constrained by the social system to act in ways that go against their
> goals. A worker who in order to feed himself and his family must perform
> the same meaningless task hundreds of times on an assembly line is likely to
> be alienated ... When a society suffers from anomie, flow is made difficult
> because it is not clear what is worth investing psychic energy in; when it suf-
> fers from alienation the problem is that one cannot invest psychic energy in
> what is clearly desirable.
>
> It is interesting to note that these two societal obstacles to flow,
> anomie and alienation, are functionally equivalent to the two personal
> pathologies, attentional disorders and self-centeredness. At both levels,
> the individual and the collective, what prevents flow from occurring is
> either the fragmentation of attentional processes (as in anomie and
> attentional disorders), or their excessive rigidity (as in alienation and self-
> centeredness). At the individual level anomie corresponds to anxiety,
> while alienation corresponds to boredom.

We need to counter these negative forces in our classrooms. When
I see kids highly engaged in the books they choose, I watch them
explore platonic and nonplatonic worlds and relationships, I watch

them develop expectations of relationships and sort through what they want or don't want in life—and maybe even start to figure out the steps to achieve it. And I see a qualitative difference between reflecting through books and reflecting through social media. The context in which you reflect matters. Privately reflecting between the pages of a book is different from publicly reflecting between social media pages. When the only audience is yourself, you are able to probe deeper and more honestly than in front of an audience of peers and family. You can suspend concern for your public image and live the questions only your heart knows. When I see kids highly engaged in social media, I see it mostly as managing their public persona, and it appears that social media can be an envy machine. They are comparatively weighing their life against others' public personas and examining their own life through the lens of others. Social networks seem to drive people apart just as frequently as they bring people together. It is not about being unilaterally against social media and video games—it's about establishing a counterbalance to all this external reflection dominating our kids' lives. We need to restore the space for the important "inner work" that needs to happen.

The French phrase *mise en abyme* describes a hall-of-mirrors effect. Reflections of reflections of reflections. It translates to English as "placing in the abyss." I can't help but conjure up a vision of our kids spending endless time staring into their personal, handheld, reflective abyss. A hall of mirrors and digital life are both confusing forms of entrapment. Instead of being guided by a coherent singular voice, who is consistent and guides you through a story, digital life, in some respects, gives you chaos: a hall of mirrors where no one is in charge. Random opinions, no matter how ill-considered, no matter how insincere or intentionally inflammatory, have an equal platform. I think we inherently crave trustworthy narration in our stories, but digital life many times gives us instead a shape-shifting rogue.

Your life has only so much mental bandwidth, and using valuable mental bandwidth to manage your online persona is going to reduce that urgent "inner work" bandwidth. Book life develops "the thread" of Stafford's poem, while social media is heavily concerned with shining the exterior shell, the public image. In a zero-sum game, we need to provide the proper balance for our children.

We need to counter the anomie and isolation of the digital world by providing social reading experiences, giving our kids in reality the solid community that social media is attempting to replicate. The social literacy of in-person peers and in-person mentors provides secure, trustworthy attachments that can never be found in the ethereal world of social media. That is the reason kids love to discuss and recommend books: so friends can read them and discuss them in person. That is a solid discussion rather than a hollow online discussion about the books. Hollow community is better than no community, but it's no match for solid community. A balance of private literary reflection and social literary engagement is what we need to create in the classroom.

We will continue to be seduced by screens, and ingenious digital ways to capture our attention will continue to proliferate. The odds are already stacked so greatly in favor of digital life that, without a school intervention, things will only get worse. A few homes with adult passion-readers will produce a few new passion-readers, but schools need to be the academy of passion-reading. Too many of our kids are not presented with an alternative to the hollow aspects of our culture. Too many of our kids get only the drudgery of skill-based testing in school and a wasteland of media at home.

When we reduce our children's living experience to the instant gratification of a screen, we are reducing our capacity to build deeper, more complex webs of knowledge and also deeper, more complete relationships with the actual people in our lives. The slow gratification of books and the slow gratification of real-world relationships are worth the extra effort. Everyone suffers when our kids focus on dry skill practice in school and absorb the media's chronicle of disaster. You can gain more nuanced perspectives and arrive at more empathic conclusions through literature. Books teach values. If children read books in school and we respect them enough to let them choose their own books, books will win, because books make a stronger, richer argument. We need to make sure we promote the message in schools with rich narratives displaying solid values—taking us on honest, funny, empathic journeys of understanding others. All stories are not created equal. If literature is given an equal shot—which it must be—literature will win.

We need to recognize that the territory where we can make our greatest impact is going to be the school day. Schools need to teach our kids empathy, conversation skills, and passion-reading as a way of improving their lives. Video games and social media are not going away, and unless we provide the time and space for passion-reading to happen in school—and build on that to support it at home—then kids will never fall in love with reading. Simply encouraging reading with words is going to be ineffective. You don't stumble into healthy eating because someone simply tells you should eat healthy, and you don't stumble into passion-reading because someone simply tells you that reading is good for you. We need to create the infrastructure for the children, so that they have the opportunity to construct healthy habits. Maybe literacy needs to start with a clear Michael Pollan dictum like, "Eat food. Not too much. Mostly plants." Something like, "Read words. Not too digital. Mostly books."

The same way we build in family dinner time to eat healthy food and extend ourselves with each other, we need to build in this reflective time to eat healthy books. The observer effect tells us that the act of observation changes the behavior of the observed. Our kids need a safe, private place for them to explore themselves without the judgment of social media, A place where they can serve themselves and not their public persona. They need this kind of mindful practice, so they can temporarily quiet the ego that resides on the surface level of social media and in an unfiltered, honest way, have private time away from the public gaze to grapple with the deeper questions of life and identity.

SOCIAL LITERACY IN ACTION: A CONVERSATION WITH THE BOYS

The unscripted events in life tend to be the best. A fascinating development this past year was the fifth grade boys developing a completely original culture, which sprouted organically. By the end of the year, they were collectively obsessed with *Percy Jackson* and Greek Mythology. One boy read *Percy Jackson*, then another, and another, reaching the critical mass for it to become a distinct part of being a boy in fifth grade. By the end of the year, they were begging me to bring in books on Greek mythology and gently fighting over books from the library. If you were a boy in fifth grade, you read, loved, and discussed *Percy Jackson* in your free time. Things like this do not result from 15 minutes of silent reading per day. They happen because we flip literacy switches in our classrooms.

Before the boys left for the summer, I gathered them together to interview them about how this all came about. Here is the interview:

MR. FLANAGAN: "One very interesting thing that I saw this year was that—even though neither I, Ms. Freeman, nor Mr. Giorno talked about Greek mythology—by the end of the year, all the boys were interested in it. So that's what I want to talk about. I am curious—where did it start?"

TREVON: "It started this year when I read *The Lightning Thief* and then I read all the series. I was trying to tell people that they should read it, too, then some people started reading it—like Darius, and Cesar, and some girls, but then when I told Darius about it, we had made this thing, where we would pretend that we were gods, and then we chose gods. I was Zeus and he was Hades and then Tamir came in . . . Tamir, Isaiah, Cesar, and Jarrell came in."

MR. FLANAGAN: "What made you pick up *Percy Jackson?*"

TREVON: "I just thought I would try to read it. I was searching for a book, and then I read the back of it, and then it sounds like a good book, so I just started reading it, and then I read the whole series."

MR. FLANAGAN: "When did you start recommending it to people?"

TREVON: "On the last book, I told Darius, Isaiah, and Jarrell that they should read the book. I said it was a good book. They didn't read it just then, because they said they had books that they were reading, then they started reading it when they were done with their books."

TAMIR: "I mean, I was interested before that, because I watched the movie, but I wasn't as interested as when he said that."

DARIUS: "Well, I remember doing independent reading and it was just me and Trevon sitting next to each other, and he was like, 'Yo, you should start reading *The Lightning Thief* because I think he was reading *The Sea of Monsters* or *The Titan's Curse* or something. And I was like 'No, no, no, no. That book is corny.' I was just making fun of the book cover. And then after I finished the book I was reading, I picked it up one day, and read it. And first he warned me the beginning of the book would be boring and at the end it starts getting better and better. And then I read the series, and I recommended it to Isaiah, because I just wanted to tell somebody about it."

ISAIAH: "I started reading it because of Darius. Because he was almost done with the series, and he told me how the whole series was going. And he was right—every book in the series gets better and better each time."

CESAR: "Well, from my point of view, I had just started reading the book not too long ago, and I'm still on *The Lightning Thief*, but I'm almost done. I kind of got into Greek mythology and all this other stuff and reading the books because of Darius, because I saw they were talking about gods and all this other stuff, and then when Trevon set up that game, and I was changing different people, and I was looking at all these new things that people had."

MR. FLANAGAN: "When did you set up the game?"

TREVON: "It was at the beginning of the year. Then it was only me and Darius. Then it was Tamir and Jarrell started getting in it, and then everybody started getting in it."

EDDIE: "So, close to now, a lot of people were starting to read the book and I was like 'What's so good about the book?' and then Darius or Trevon said 'When you read the book, the books get better.' Because I thought the book looked corny, because it looked old and stuff and beaten up. I don't really like books that are beat up, because if the pages fall out, and I don't know how to like, what page..."

REGGIE: "You ever heard of page numbers?"

EDDIE: "Well, like every single page, well, not every single page, but a lot of pages fall out, and I don't have time to put them back in. So I tried to read the first book. I'm still on *The Lightning Thief*; so far it's a little boring, but I kind of like it because of how he starts out. I like a lot of the details."

TREVON: "Can I say a recommendation? There are a lot of books by Rick Riordan, and there are a lot of series, *Heroes of Olympus, Percy Jackson, The Kane Chronicles,* things like that. You should read *Percy Jackson and The Olympians* first. Percy Jackson meets the characters in *The Kane Chronicles.*"

CESAR: "This is just a quick thing, because before I read *Percy Jackson* I was reading *The Kane Chronicles,* and I had to skip the first book because I couldn't find it, so I read the first book last, and it seemed out of order, but it was still a good book and all that."

DARIUS: "If I could just make credits real quick, I'd say Trevon was like the main producer. I was like a side recommendation, and all the other people started coming, just to learn more and stuff."

MR. FLANAGAN: "What I noticed that was really interesting, for me as a teacher, is that we didn't do anything this year with Greek mythology in any classes. And all of a sudden I hear you guys talking about it outside, I hear you talking about it in the hallways, I hear you talking about it at recess, I see you trading books. And then two weeks ago, *everyone* just starts asking me do I have any books about *anything* to do with Greek mythology. You all wanted to read them—and not just the Percy Jackson books. And I was bringing in whatever I could find, and everyone was trading books, swapping books, and I brought in books and everyone was grabbing them, and wanted to read them, and I just found that amazing. It was really cool that you guys started something and how it spread throughout the whole class."

TREVON: "The Percy Jackson series I got from myself, but *Heroes of Olympus* I saw William [a sixth-grade student] reading *The Lost Hero*. And I also saw *The Lost Hero* in one of those book-order forms. And then one day Ms. Freeman knew I was a Greek mythology geek, so when she was looking at the book orders, she saw that it had *Heroes of Olympus* Books 1–4, and she said she might buy it for me, if people get a lot of books."

The conversation concluded with them explaining elements of the game they invented; how they identified with the personalities of certain gods, goddesses, demigods, or titans; the story of Prometheus; and how you have to read a certain amount of the Percy Jackson books and have a good knowledge of Greek mythology to be a member of the special council in their game. The joy these boys wove with books and camaraderie was authentic and unmistakable.

• • •

THE DIGNITY, GROWTH, AND JOY OF NARRATIVE IMMERSION

*The true opposite of obedience is not disobedience but
independence. The true opposite of order is not disorder
but freedom. The true opposite of control is not chaos but self-control.*

~ JAY GRIFFITHS

angibles may make life possible, but intangibles make life worth living. Well-written stories provide shape to abstractions like wonder, love, compassion, humor, determination, and existential integrity. These lessons can be delivered by an effective educational framework at our immediate disposal—the combination of joy, narrative, and camaraderie. When we deny our children this potent combination in school, we are denying the very things that make us human. When you read for extended periods of time about what directly concerns you and share this with a community that cares for one another, you are not getting dry skills taught in a purposeless vacuum, but countless authentic lessons backed with an emotional grip.

If reading is ever to survive school, it needs an incubation period of warm auditory modeling. Studying rules and practicing drills don't inspire additional practice or motivation. We need the camaraderie, the laughter, the fun. We need the space, time, and freedom to play. We need to create positive feedback loops initiated by immediate access to well-written, high-interest stories. We need to prioritize giving students considerable self-directed, authentic reading practice time every single day. Students thrive when they are given a clear purpose, proper support, and autonomy. Joy of the game will facilitate the drive to practice, which will improve performance. Life without joy isn't much of a life, and a school without joy isn't much of a school. Joy and storytelling need to be at the core of our instruction.

We are novelty-seeking storytellers, and we should be spending class time engaged in complete, autotelic experiences. Interrupting that flow to administer tests excessively, to interfere, to measure some quasi-technical progress, to stigmatize with norm-referenced performance against precocious peers only diminishes motivation and impedes growth. It is counterproductive. Measurement of that time only corrupts the existential beauty of that time.

When we deny children access to high-quality reading experiences, time to read, and freedom to pursue the pressing questions that they have, we are denying them a path to a successful life. We need to create the time and space for them to follow that path. Function-reading is about a meager utility, while passion-reading is about ingenuity. If we can succeed in turning a function-reader into a passion-reader, we can not only give someone the ability to find success but also a lifelong portable sanctuary in a frequently daunting world.

If we agree with Jay Griffiths, and genuinely seek to cultivate independence, freedom, and self-control within our children, then we need to afford them the trust and respect they need to accomplish those things. Investigating what is personally significant should be a human right.

And it is a right that many of our children are denied. How can we expect kids ever to love reading without providing for genuinely joyous reading experiences? How can you love something to which you have never been properly introduced? And if, as Yeats says, education is not the filling of a pail, but the lighting of a fire, then we need to stop trying to kindle fires with soggy worksheets. We need schools to operate less like fire departments and more like storytelling arsonists.

The most effective use of your limited classroom time is trying to turn students into lifelong passion-readers. That is the ultimate educational multiplier. That is the way to change a child's life in measurable and immeasurable ways. You are teaching the child to be his or her own best teacher and how to answer the questions only their heart knows. Craving stories is elemental, and kids will find stories to make meaning of their life and their world, whether they find those stories at school in well-considered read-alouds and books, or on their own in the suspect world of popular media. The least we can do is provide sufficient exposure to what Philip Pullman deems "superior stories"—stories that encourage resourcefulness, determination, and improvement of ourselves and our world. We need to respect kids enough and afford them the same dignity that we expect as adults—the acknowledgment that our specific personal interests matter.

Passion-readers realize that they have an infinite variety of experiences at their fingertips. They realize reading is the constructor of dreams and destroyer of false boundaries. They know that the problems they have likely have solutions, if only they know where to look. They know that they can benefit from the boundless diversity of human wisdom to which only readers have access. They know that when dreams become insolvent, you create new ones. They know they can explore impossible places and satisfy their deepest curiosities about the world. They realize that reading changes you in inexpressible ways, that reading can comfort us, that stories can be there for us when we don't have anyone else who understands us. They realize that reading thickens the thread that is the core of who we are. They triangulate who they are from the stories of others, gaining irreplaceable value and perspective. Passion-readers grasp the paradox of how intimately unique their own story is, yet how much it has in common with all human stories. They realize "the other" is not all that other. They realize that their questions have been asked for thousands of years and that by choosing the right books, they might just live their way into the answers.

Narrative immersion provides you with context about your place in the world. You realize that whatever your struggles may be, you are not alone, and that you are part of a larger circle of life. Knowing that other people have lived through what you have lived through is empowering, and their stories may even light a path forward. One of the greatest lessons reading has to teach is that normal, everyday people are capable of changing the world. It can help demystify the superficial, high-gloss world of media presentation and show the normalcy of the self-doubt, missteps, and flawed nature of people who nonetheless make a difference. Reading teaches us to approach life with what Martin Luther King Jr. called "creative maladjustment": not passively accepting the problems of the world but instead attempting to address and correct injustice in inventive, positive ways.

We are producers and consumers of stories, sustained by joy and camaraderie. And we need to show regard for students by dignifying their unique personal passions and allowing the space for them to pursue their curiosity. We all want our students to work hard, become proficient readers, and have a thriving intellectual life, and we can accomplish these things when we intertwine the imaginative power of story with thousands of hours of joyous, deliberate practice. Stories are where we extend our search for experience. Growth is extension, and curiosity is self-determined extension. Student extension cannot be imposed, only cultivated. When we teach reading as a utilitarian function, it's bloodless. It's epistemically unsound, and it's a foundation antithetical to growth and freedom. It's an ephemeral maneuver suited for placating extrinsic demands. When we teach reading as the curiosity-driven, essential pursuit of meaning, we empower students to initiate themselves in self-determination.

Students cannot indefinitely tread on static surfaces. We can help diminish unnecessary suffering in the classroom, with its mind-numbing tedium and debilitating effect on morale, by harnessing innate curiosity and providing students the supportive freedom to reach, extend, and determine their destinations. We can expose them to a diverse array of thought and perspective. We can expand imaginations and build authentic relationships during read-aloud sessions, and we can raise our students reading proficiency with intensive, engaging daily practice. We can blunt inequality with immediate access to high-quality storytelling through well-curated collections and professional actors modeling prosodic narration. And we can immerse students in the superior stories: the stories that teach us not to be idle and wait to be saved but to save ourselves through determination, creativity, and resourcefulness; the stories that tell us not to pass our time in the dark, but to satisfy our compulsion to explore; the stories that teach us that light doesn't uncover itself through shadows, but if you expand yourself, you may find radiance; the honest stories that reflect our grim world, but also reveal that it is neither sealed nor immovable.

• • •

ABOUT THE AUTHOR

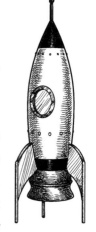

James Flanagan, MA Ed., teaches English and Language Arts in the School District of Philadelphia. He also conducts practitioner research focusing on engagement, high-volume reading, choice, and prosodic audiobook modeling. He has contributed to the *Journal of Adolescent & Adult Literacy*, *The Writing Teacher's Companion*, and *Literacy Today*, and also copresented at the International Literacy Association's National Conference. James has been a reading teacher in Philadelphia since 2002.

Made in the USA
Middletown, DE
16 August 2021

45382840R00104